THE WHOLE EARTH HOLIDAY BOOK

Linda Polon and Aileen Cantwell

Scott, Foresman and Company
Glenview, Illinois
Dallas, Texas   Oakland, New Jersey
Palo Alto, California   Tucker, Georgia
London

More GOOD YEAR® Books in Language Arts and Reading

BASICS AND BEYOND
Practical Writing Activities for Today and Tomorrow
Michelle Berman and Linda Shevitz

BIG BOOK OF WRITING
Sandra Kaplan, Sheila Madsen, Bette T. Gould

DO YOU READ ME?
Practical Approaches to Teaching Reading Comprehension
Arnold A. Griese

GALAXY OF GAMES
For Reinforcing Writing Skills
Jerry Mallett

GETTING THE MOST OUT OF TELEVISION
Dorothy Singer, Jerome Singer, Diana M. Zuckerman

GETTING READY TO READ
Volume 1 and 2
Harry W. Forgan and M. Liz Christman-Rothlein

I CAN MAKE IT ON MY OWN
Functional Reading Ideas and Activities for Daily Survival
Michelle Berman and Linda Shevitz

IMAGINE THAT!
Illustrated Poems and Creative Learning Experiences
Joyce King and Carol Katzman

LANGUAGE ARTS IDEA BOOK
Classroom Activities for Children
Joanne Schaff

MAKING KIDS CLICK
Independent Activities in Reading and Language Arts
Linda Polon and Aileen Cantwell

ME? TEACH READING?
Activities for Secondary Content Area Teachers
Mary Beth Culp and Sylvia Spann

NEW DIMENSIONS IN ENGLISH
An Ideabook of Language Arts Activities for Middle and Secondary School Teachers
Joanne Schaff

OUNCE OF PREVENTION PLUS A POUND OF CURE
Tests and Techniques for Aiding Individual Readers
Ronald W. Burton

PHORGAN'S PHONICS
Harry W. Forgan

READ ALL ABOUT IT
Using Interests and Hobbies to Motivate Young Readers
Harry W. Forgan

READING CORNER
Ideas, Games, And Activities for Individualizing Reading
Harry W. Forgan

READING FOR SURVIVAL IN TODAY'S SOCIETY
Volumes I and II
Anne H. Adams, Anne Flowers, and Elsa E. Woods

READING ROUSERS
114 Ways to Reading Fun
Marian Bartch and Jerry Mallett

SPECIAL THINGS FOR SPECIAL DAYS
Pat Short and Billee Davidson

SUCCESS IN READING AND WRITING SERIES
Anne H. Adams, Elizabeth Bebensee, Helen Cappleman, Judith Connors, and Mary Johnson

TEACHER'S CHOICE
Ideas and Activities for Teaching Basic Skills
Sandra N. Kaplan, Sheila K. Madsen, and Bette T. Gould

TOTALACTION
Ideas and Activities for Teaching Children Ages Five to Eight
Pat Short and Billee Davidson

WRITE UP A STORM
Creative Writing Ideas and Activities for the Middle Grades
Linda Polon and Aileen Cantwell

WRITING CORNER
Arnold Cheyney

For information about these or other GOOD YEAR® Books, please write to

GOOD YEAR® Books
Scott, Foresman and Company
1900 East Lake Avenue
Glenview, Illinois 60025

ISBN: 0-673-16585-X

Copyright © 1983 Scott, Foresman and Company.

Printed in the United States of America.

123456 MAL 888786858483

Contents

Preface

Children love holidays. What, then, could they find more fascinating than joining in the celebrations of scores of holidays from around the world?

The Whole Earth Holiday Book is packed with stories and activity worksheets that you can use to introduce a wide variety of cultures as well as to sharpen your students' language arts skills. Each story explains a holiday's history and customs. Each worksheet reinforces reading comprehension through a challenging puzzle format. In addition, many holidays offer ideas for creative writing assignments.

Just think of the many ways in which you can use these holiday units:

- Teach a guided reading lesson to the entire class, with each child having his or her own story sheet. Assist with the activity worksheet if necessary.
- Assign a story/activity unit as an independent project, either as a supplement to the regular program or as a homework assignment.
- Set up a decorated center around a particular holiday. You can project and enlarge the art in this book on a sheet of tagboard via an opaque or overhead projector.
- Create a monthly center featuring the coming holidays. Change the story sheets as the school year advances.
- Build a class study unit around a single holiday with art, music, dance, and reading activities. Your local library has many resource books for multicultural holiday projects.
- Develop an entire social studies unit devoted to international holidays. You can use the holiday celebrations in this book as a starting point for encouraging children to learn about countries and customs around the world.

While all the foreign words in *The Whole Earth Holiday Book* are defined in the text, you may want to introduce some words — like "feast," "eve," and "traditional" — that are basic to the meaning of holidays and that appear frequently throughout the stories and activities.

We have tried to include popular and representative holidays in *The Whole Earth Holiday Book*. Since every day is a holiday in some part of the world, we naturally couldn't accommodate all of them. And since celebrations of the same holiday can differ within a country or a culture — often depending on how religious the celebrants happen to be — we couldn't describe in detail the full range of observances for every holiday we included.

We're nonetheless confident that you'll find *The Whole Earth Holiday Book* an enriching and enjoyable experience for you and your students.

To Genie Shapiro for her love of children everywhere and to Mary Cantwell and Marty Polon for their support and love.

And special thanks to...
    the Japanese, Spanish, and German consuls
    Ngoc Bach
    Hea-Young Yoon Kuhn
    Mary Jeanne Lewis
    Ella Kato
    Susan Lewis
    Susan Duck
    Alice Gilbert

Labor Day

Imagine a holiday that honors hard-working people. Since 1894, the United States has set aside the first Monday in September as Labor Day. It's a day of rest for America's workers.

At first, Labor Day wasn't a holiday for everyone. Only those people called laborers — mostly factory workers — got the day off. These workers usually put in long, tiring hours at their jobs. And they didn't earn much money.

There might never have been a Labor Day holiday if not for Peter J. McGuire. He was the leader of the Knights of Labor, an early labor organization. In 1882, Mr. McGuire suggested that the United States put aside one day a year to honor working people.

Shortly after Mr. McGuire's suggestion, the first Labor Day parade was held in New York City's Union Square. On September 5, 1882, thousands of people took the day off from their jobs to march in the parade, attend picnics, and set off fireworks. They made speeches about better working conditions in the United States. They called for a shorter work day and for higher wages. The Knights of Labor decided to celebrate Labor Day every year.

But Labor Day has changed greatly over the last 100 years. Now it has become a family holiday for all Americans, not just factory workers. And instead of making speeches, most people celebrate the holiday by going on camping trips or to sporting events or just enjoying a last three-day weekend before the new school year begins.

Many towns and cities across the United States have their own Labor Day celebrations. For example, in the town of Henryella, Oklahoma, there are dune buggy races and turtle races — along with a band concert and picnic — to celebrate Labor Day. Morgan City, Louisiana celebrates on both land and water. On land, a king and queen of the Labor Day parade receive their crowns amid fireworks. Then they view such royal entertainment as a swimming meet, a square dance, and a football jamboree. On water, the shrimp fleet receives the blessing of the community. People pray for the protection of the boats and crews.

Many other countries have a labor day holiday, too. But they usually celebrate the holiday on May 1, the traditional May Day. Canada is the only other country that celebrates on the same day as the United States.

Labor Day

Can you make your way from "Start School" to "Take The Day Off"? The numbers of the true statements below can guide you safely. Circle the number of each true statement, and then trace your successful path with a pencil through the Labor Day maze. But be careful! The false statements will get you lost.

1. The Labor Day holiday goes back 100 years.

2. In 1894, Labor Day became a legal holiday.

3. Workers never spent long days at their jobs.

4. The first Labor Day parade was held on September 5, 1882.

5. Mr. McGuire was head of Hard Workers of America.

6. Labor Day is a day of rest for working people.

7. Other countries have a labor day holiday, too.

8. On Labor Day, people are supposed to catch up on their work.

9. Very few U.S. towns hold Labor Day celebrations.

10. Peter J. McGuire came up with the idea for Labor Day.

11. A long time ago, workers earned lots of money.

12. Early Labor Day celebrations never had marches, speeches, or picnics.

13. People today never relax on Labor Day.

14. On the first Labor Day, workers made speeches.

15. Labor Day is the first Monday in September.

16. The first Labor Day parade took place in Maryland.

17. Workers never wanted a shorter work day.

18. Labor Day is celebrated in some countries on May 1.

19. Today, Labor Day is a family holiday.

Start School

2
5
4
9
8
14
10
6
7
11
15   16
12
1
13
17
18
3
19

Take The Day Off

The Ramadan Fast and Id-Ul-Fitr

In Jordan, Pakistan, Morocco, Syria, and other Moslem countries, people watch for the full moon of late summer or early fall. When it appears, the Ramadan fast begins. For the next month, Moslem people will not eat, drink, or smoke from sunrise to sunset. They will spend their days praying in mosques.

For more than 1300 years, Moslems have fasted during Ramadan in memory of their prophet Mohammed. The Moslem holy book, the Koran, teaches that fasting and prayer quiet the spirit and discipline the soul. During Ramadan, Moslems everywhere enjoy a feeling of togetherness.

As the holy month of fasting draws to an end, people stand on rooftops to search the sky for the next full moon. When they see it, their shouts and cries join the beating of drums to announce the beginning of a three-day festival know as *Id-Ul-Fitr.* It is time to end the Ramadan fast and begin the family celebration. *Id* means "happiness"; *Fitr* means "breaking the fast."

On the first morning of *Id-Ul-Fitr,* Moslems travel to brightly lighted mosques to pray. When the priests call out, "Allah is great," the worshippers bend forward on prayer mats, raise their hands high, and press their heads against the ground. Then they greet one another saying, "Id Mubarak" which means "happiness to everyone."

When they return from the mosque, families gather for the first midday meal in a month. They enjoy a dish called *saiwiyan* — thin noodles cooked with milk, sugar, and coconut. Other favorites include tender lamb, juicy goat meat, and vegetables in spicy sauces. For dessert there is a candy made of ground nuts, honey, sesame seeds, and grated cheese.

Children receive plenty of attention during *Id-Ul-Fitr.* Mothers make or buy new clothes for them. Girls wear bangles around their wrists and paint beautiful red designs on their hands.

Since most people don't work during the holiday celebration, families spend time together. Parents take their children to fairs, for strolls through the streets, and on shopping trips to special holiday stands. At the fairs, children can watch puppet shows as well as play on swings, merry-go-rounds, and ferris wheels. In the evening, colorful fireworks explode under the stars.

On the last day of *Id-Ul-Fitr,* families visit relatives and friends. It is at this time, too, that parents give coins and other gifts to their children.

The Ramadan Fast
and Id-Ul-Fitr

What do children do with their pets during the *Id-Ul-Fitr* celebration? To find out, decide whether the following statements are true or false. Then circle the letter under "True" or "False" for each statement. Place the circled letters — in order — on the blanks at the bottom of the page. The first one has been done for you.

		True	False
1.	*Id* means "anxious," and *Fitr* means "unbroken."	m	(p)
2.	The Koran is the Moslems' holy book.	a	o
3.	Ramadan and *Id-Ul-Fitr* are celebrated in countries where there are no Moslems.	e	i
4.	Moslems eat, drink, and smoke from sunrise to sunset during Ramadan.	m	n
5.	The Ramadan fast began in memory of Mohammed.	t	w
6.	A half moon starts the Ramadan fast and *Id-Ul-Fitr*.	d	c
7.	*Id Mubarak* means "happiness to all."	o	a
8.	Allah is the Moslem god.	l	s
9.	During *Id-Ul-Fitr,* girls paint designs on their ankles.	a	o
10.	The beating of drums tells everyone that the fast of Ramadan has started.	p	r
11.	Syrians do not celebrate the Ramadan fast.	v	r
12.	The Ramadan fast gives Moslems everywhere a feeling of togetherness.	a	o
13.	A favorite dish during *Id-Ul-Fitr* is a food called *saiwiyan*.	i	e
14.	Moslems pray in mosques during the fast.	n	f
15.	The Ramadan fast and *Id-Ul-Fitr* are new holidays.	g	b
16.	The Ramadan fast and *Id-Ul-Fitr* are based on the Earth's movements around the sun.	e	o
17.	Children wear new clothes during *Id-Ul-Fitr*.	w	m
18.	During *Id-Ul-Fitr,* families spend little time together.	c	d
19.	Moslems shout for joy when the full moon appears and *Id-Ul-Fitr* begins.	r	y
20.	Children receive gifts on the last day of *Id-Ul-Fitr*.	e	c
21.	Moslems sit on chairs while praying in mosques.	h	s
22.	Moslems eat their first lunch after the Ramadan fast on the second day of *Id-Ul-Fitr*.	r	s

Children p __ __ __ __ their pets every __ __ __ __ __
          1 2 3 4 5   6 7 8 9 10

in the __ __ __ __ __ __ __ to __ __ __ __ __ them up.
      11 12 13 14 15 16 17   18 19 20 21 22

Mid-Autumn Festival
Tết-Trung-Thu

Mid-Autumn Festival, or *Tết-Trung-Thu,* is a time of joy for Vietnamese children. The exact day of the celebration varies with the lunar calendar, but it is usually around September 15, during the eighth lunar month.

Some people say that *Tết-Trung-Thu* began long, long ago. Emperor Minh-Mang fell asleep in his garden, and he dreamed that a fairy took him to the moon. There he met a beautiful queen. He saw a graceful dance in her honor and ate cakes shaped like the moon. When the emperor awoke, he felt sad that he had only been dreaming. So he taught his servants to do the moon dance, and he asked them to bake moon cakes. Ever since then, the Vietnamese have had an annual celebration of the moon.

There is another story about the beginning of this festival. The people of Vietnam base their calendar on the movements of the moon, and they watch the moon's motion and shape very carefully. Some people say that *Tết-Trung-Thu* began during the eighth month of the year because that is when the moon looks fullest and most beautiful.

No matter how *Tết-Trung-Thu* got started, it is a holiday for imagination and romance. Teenagers and adults fall in love while gazing at the bright moon. But the Mid-Autumn Festival is mostly for Vietnamese children. Boys and girls buy or build colorful lanterns in the shapes of rabbits, fish, birds, unicorns, dragons, boats, or moons. Inside each lantern they place a picture that tells a story from Vietnamese legends. Poor children decorate soda pop cans and put candles inside to make their Mid-Autumn Festival lanterns.

On festival night, children dance and parade through the streets. They swing their lanterns to music and pretend that they are taking a trip to the moon. Since Vietnamese children do not have many toys, the festival lanterns are especially important to them.

Before and after the parade, children and adults munch on a special treat — moon cakes. Moon cakes are round and flat and filled with a mixture of pork, watermelon seeds, shark fins, and sugar. Some are filled with black beans mashed with sugar. Bakeries sell the fresh, sweet moon cakes, and people bake them at home, too.

Long ago, women and girls held moon cake contests during *Tết-Trung-Thu.* People said that the unmarried girl who made the best moon cake would have no trouble finding a husband.

Today, parents carve sugar canes into tiny chairs or mold grapefruit slices into animal shapes for their children. No one knows for sure how or why these customs began, but Vietnamese children love every part of the Mid-Autumn Festival.

Mid-Autumn Festival
Tết-Trung-Thu

Make up a question about the Mid-Autumn Festival to go with each of the answers given below. The first one is done for you.

1. Q: What is another name for the Mid-Autumn Festival?
   A: *Tết-Trung-Thu*

2. Q: _____
   _____?
   A: Emperor Minh-Mang

3. Q: _____
   _____?
   A: Moon cakes

4. Q: _____
   _____?
   A: Movements of the moon

5. Q: _____
   _____?
   A: September 15

6. Q: _____
   _____?
   A: Lanterns

7. Q: _____
   _____?
   A: Make-believe trip to the moon

8. Q: _____
   _____?
   A: Dance and parade

9. Q: _____
   _____?
   A: Grapefruit slices

10. Q: _____
    _____?
    A: Fall in love

11. Q: _____
    _____?
    A: Celebration of the moon

12. Q: _____
    _____?
    A: Round and flat

On another piece of paper, design a lantern for the Mid-Autumn Festival. Draw a picture to go inside the lantern, and write a legend that tells about the picture inside your *Tết-Trung-Thu* lantern.

Mexican Independence Day

Every morning a priest named Miguel Hidalgo would ring the bell in his church. The people of his parish were used to hearing the bell. But on the morning of September 16, 1810, they heard something unusual. As Father Hidalgo rang the bell that morning he shouted, *"¡Viva la Independencia! ¡Viva Mexico!"*

Father Hidalgo's cry for Mexican independence started a long fight for freedom from Spain. His words (called *El Grito de Dolores)* spread all over Mexico. He tried to lead a Mexican war for independence. But in 1811 he was captured by the Spanish and shot as a traitor.

Today, Miguel Hidalgo is remembered as the Father of Mexican Independence. And the Mexican people celebrate his famous shout on September 16 as Mexican Independence Day. Every year the president of Mexico rings the very same bell that Father Hidalgo rang in 1810, and the president repeats *El Grito de Dolores.*

To show pride in their country on Independence Day, Mexicans fly the flag and sing the national anthem, *"Mexicanos, al Grito de Guerra."* In each city and town, crowds gather in the *zócalo* (town square). Flags and wreaths of flowers drape the buildings. Confetti and paper streamers fly everywhere.

Some towns add still more noise and color with a *torito.* A *torito* is a little toy bull made of wire, paper, and straw. Attached to the toy are firecrackers, sparklers, and pinwheels. A boy carries the *torito* on his shoulders, and as he dashes through the streets, sparks go shooting in every direction.

One of the big events of Mexican Independence Day is the National Lottery. Because the lottery tickets are so inexpensive, almost everyone can buy a chance to win the top prize. The lucky person who wins becomes an instant millionaire! The winning ticket is drawn from a gigantic container in Mexico City. But nearly everyone in Mexico watches on television or listens to the radio to see who will win. The Lottery helps bring Mexicans together as they celebrate their Independence Day holiday.

Mexican Independence Day

Inside the small bells are words that deal with Mexican Independence Day. Use these words to write a brief explanation of what the holiday is all about.

bell
Spain
¡Viva Mexico!
September 16
Father Hidalgo

_____

_____

_____

_____

_____

_____

_____

_____

_____

flag
torito
fiesta
fireworks
National Lottery
President of Mexico

Inside the large bells are two story ideas. Pick one of the ideas and write a short story about it on a separate sheet of paper.

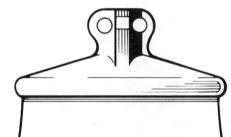

Imagine how excited you would be to win Mexico's Independence Day Lottery. Suppose you received an envelope in the mail a few days before the Lottery drawing. Inside was a single ticket. You had no idea who sent it. Then on September 16 you got a telegram that said you had won the top prize! Write a story about the mysterious ticket that made you a millionaire. Don't forget to mention how you spent your prize money.

It is September 16, and you have been chosen for a special honor. You are to carry the *torito* (little bull) on your shoulders in the town's fiesta. You have a problem, though. You are afraid of fireworks. Nobody knows about your fear, and all your friends keep telling you how lucky you are. Write a story about the fiesta and how you solved your problem.

American Indian Day

The purpose of American Indian Day is to honor the traditions of the many great Indian nations in the United States. The first group to observe American Indian Day were the Boy Scouts of New York State.

In 1914, a member of the Montana Blackfoot Nation — Red Fox James — campaigned for a national holiday to honor American Indians. He traveled across the United States on horseback (more than 4,000 miles!) to win the support of state governors.

Soon after, the American Indian Association backed the movement for an American Indian Day. And in 1916, New York officially proclaimed the holiday. Today, some states observe American Indian Day on the fourth Saturday in September, others on the second Saturday in May.

More than half of the almost one million American Indians now live on reservations. On American Indian Day we remember Indians of the past, and we honor the heritage they left us.

Cochise

Cochise was a great leader of the Apache Indians, who lived in the southwestern part of the United States. When another group of Apaches kidnapped the son of an Arizona rancher, an army officer blamed Cochise. The officer approached under a white flag of truce, but then he arrested Cochise and several Apache warriors.

Cochise escaped and led a long war against the United States Army. Finally, Captain T.J. Jeffords — a trusted friend and blood brother of Cochise — helped make peace. The Apaches were promised that they could remain on their own land.

Only a few months later, however, the promise was broken. The bloody fighting went on until General O.O. Howard accepted Cochise's demand for an Apache reservation on Apache territory.

Geronimo

Geronimo had been an Apache leader since his youth. His life was peaceful until one day Mexican soldiers rode through the Apache camp killing many women and children — including Geronimo's mother, wife, and three children. He could think of nothing but revenge. Geronimo led his warriors on many raids in northern Mexico, killing everywhere they went.

After Cochise died, the U.S. Government tried to move the Apaches away from the Southwest. Geronimo, angry at seeing his people betrayed again, went on the warpath once more. He brought terror and death to settlements on both sides of the Mexican-U.S. border.

After many battles, though, Geronimo was forced to surrender. The Apaches then moved from their homeland to a reservation in Florida. Geronimo was the last great Apache chief.

Chief Joseph

The Nez Percé Indians had always been on good terms with the explorers and settlers who crossed their land. In 1805, the Indians welcomed the Lewis and Clark Expedition, and they lived in peace with the settlers who followed. The settlers promised the Nez Percé that the Wallowa Valley in Oregon would always stay Indian land.

As more white settlers came into Oregon, however, many promises were broken. At times, Indians were murdered and their cattle and land stolen. Yet the Nez Percé — under the leadership of Chief Joseph — kept the peace.

Even when General Howard ordered the Nez Percé to a reservation, Chief Joseph was willing to obey. He did not want to see his people killed. Some of his warriors, however, defied their chief. They killed 18 settlers. Chief Joseph was outraged at his warriors. Nevertheless, he decided that he had no choice but to go to war with the U.S. Army.

Many battles followed. Chief Joseph hoped to unite all the Indians of the Northwest, but his dream never came true. Forced to retreat, he led his people more than 1,500 miles — twice over the Rocky Mountains! — in an attempt to reach safety in Canada. Just 30 miles from the border, however, Chief Joseph and his people were surrounded and forced to surrender.

In 1878, Chief Joseph went to Washington, D.C. to plead for his people. No one listened to him. The Nez Percé were moved to a reservation in Oklahoma and then back to the Northwest. Chief Joseph tried to look after his people, but he died a sad and disappointed man.

American Indian Day

Cochise, Geronimo, and Chief Joseph were three great American Indian leaders. Fill in the important facts about each of them in the profiles below.

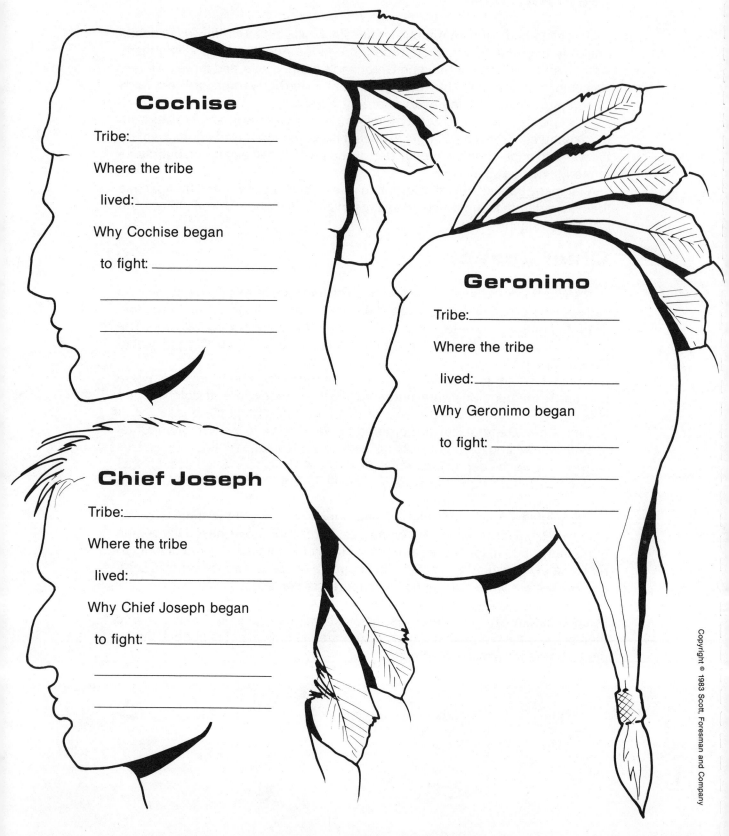

Cochise

Tribe:_____

Where the tribe

lived:_____

Why Cochise began

to fight: _____

_____

_____

Geronimo

Tribe:_____

Where the tribe

lived:_____

Why Geronimo began

to fight: _____

_____

_____

Chief Joseph

Tribe:_____

Where the tribe

lived:_____

Why Chief Joseph began

to fight: _____

_____

_____

American Indian Day

All three of these great American Indian leaders shared some things in common. Fill in the missing words on the blanks below. Then add the missing letters in the vertical boxes to name the place where Cochise, Geronimo, and Chief Joseph died.

1. Each was the leader of his .... — ☐ — — —

2. Each was unhappy due to a broken .... — — — — — ☐ —

3. At first, each wanted to be the new settlers' ..... — ☐ — — — —

4. Each one fought without................................. — — ☐ — —

5. None of them really wanted to .... — ☐ — — —

6. Each wanted to keep his own .... — — ☐ —

Chusongnal

Chusongnal is the Korean day of thanksgiving. The word *"Chusongnal"* means "autumn night" in Chinese, and the holiday is usually celebrated in September.

All the Korean people celebrate *Chusongnal,* but it is a special holiday for the farmers. To them it means a day of rest after the long, weary days of the rice harvest. A farmers' band moves from one village to the next, playing at each festival. The musicians wear long ribbons tied around their heads. As they beat their drums and clang their cymbals, they shake their heads so that the colorful ribbons keep time to the music. In the cities, people celebrate *Chusongnal* by visiting friends and exchanging gifts of food.

It is on *Chusongnal* that the Korean people remember their ancestors. Families visit cemeteries to honor the spirits of the dead and to ask their ancestors' blessing on the food from the harvest. At home, they hold another ceremony honoring their ancestors. Called *tschare,* the ceremony is an offering of five foods of five different colors: dates, apples, chestnuts, pears, and persimmons.

For their thanksgiving feasts, families gather around a low table and sit on *bahnsuk* (cushions). When guests are present, children often sit at a separate table as a sign of respect. Good manners are extremely important in Korean homes. Each child bows to parents and grandparents before sitting down. Then the children wait to eat until the oldest person at the table picks up the chopsticks. On special occasions like *Chusongnal,* the Korean people often use chopsticks made of silver.

The *Chusongnal* table is filled with a great variety of foods: fried beef on skewers, chicken, pork, fish, vegetables, fruit, and *song pyun. Song pyun* are rice cakes make into the shape of half-moons. Long ago, it was traditional for men to beat the rice dough with large wooden hammers. Today, most Korean families get their *song pyun* from a bakery, or women prepare the cakes at home.

All Korean meals feature *kimchee.* A favorite treat made of cabbage or cucumbers mixed with radishes, hot peppers, garlic, and ginger, *kimchee* is a very spicy dish.

The Korean day of thanksgiving ends with a traditional holiday song, *Kang Kang Suwolle.* Girls join in a circle dance as they sing the song, which asks the moon for good luck. It is a happy way to end *Chusongnal.*

Chusongnal

The words in the sentences below have been scrambled. Put the words in the right order on the blanks. When you have finished, copy the circled words at the bottom of the page to reveal a secret message about the holiday. The first sentence has been done for you.

1. September Korean thanksgiving (The) is day in of

   The Korean day of thanksgiving is in September.

2. honor their (People) ancestors

   _____ _____ _____ _____.

3. parents bow Children a to (give) their

   _____ _____ _____ _____ _____ _____ _____.

4. give for harvest People a good (thanks)

   _____ _____ _____ _____ – _____ _____.

5. member family around a sits (Each) table low

   _____ _____ _____ _____ _____ – _____ _____.

6. (year) farmers' a plays Every band

   _____ _____ _____ – _____ _____.

7. are shape Rice cakes half of a moon the (in)

   _____ _____ _____ _____ _____ – _____ _____ – _____.

8. special (Korea) a is kimchee treat In

   __ _____, _____ _____ _____ _____.

9. day exchange of food gifts Friends this (on)

   _____ _____ _____ _____ _____ _____ _____ _____.

10. (Chusongnal) and dancing Music part of are

    _____ _____ _____ _____ _____ _____.

Your Holiday Secret Message:

The _____ _____ _____ _____ _____

_____ – _____ – _____ _____.

Rosh Hashanah and Yom Kippur

To the Jewish people of long, long ago, the gathering of the harvest meant the end of one year and the beginning of the next. The High Holy Days of *Rosh Hashanah* and *Yom Kippur* began as a harvest festival. They are still celebrated as they were centuries ago in the middle of September or October — harvest time.

But now the High Holy Days are a time for welcoming the new year by thinking about wrongdoings done over the past year and praying for God's forgiveness. People attend services at temples or synagogues. At the services, they think about how they will behave in the coming year, especially how they can be more thoughtful toward others.

The High Holy Days last for ten days. The first two days are *Rosh Hashanah.* The tenth day is *Yom Kippur.* The holiday period begins at sundown on the first day of *Rosh Hashanah.* The family has a special holiday meal. During the meal they dip *hallah* (a kind of bread) in honey and say a blessing that asks for a sweet year ahead. Sometimes the *hallah* is round to symbolize the whole year. Sometimes it looks like a braided ladder to help prayers rise to God. Another favorite holiday food is *tsimmes,* a dish made of sweet potatoes, meat, prunes, and carrots.

At the temples and synagogues, a ram's horn — called a *shofar* — is blown at the beginning of the *Rosh Hashanah* services. Jews believe that their names are written in the Book of Life with a list of their good and their bad deeds. During the High Holy Days, God opens the book so that people can correct their wrongdoings before the Book is closed again. *Rosh Hashanah* is a happy time. People smile, shake hands, and exchange greeting cards to wish one another a happy new year.

Yom Kippur is a more solemn time. *Yom Kippur* means "Day of Atonement," and Jews try to cleanse themselves of sins. Many fast from sunset to sunset, not eating, drinking, or smoking for a full 24 hours. The fasting is a way of cleansing the body to symbolize the cleansing of the soul. At the end of *Yom Kippur,* one long blast of the ram's horn is the signal that the High Holy Days have concluded.

For Jews, the *Rosh Hashanah* and *Yom Kippur* holidays are a time to remember the past and hope for the future.

Rosh Hashanah and Yom Kippur

Each sentence below has one word with its letters scrambled. Figure out what each word is supposed to be, and put the letters in the boxes in the right order. Then enter each circled letter on the correct blank at the bottom of the next page. The first sentence is done for you.

When you're finished, you'll find that the message at the bottom of the page spells out the meaning of *Rosh Hashanah.*

1. *Rosh Hashanah* is still 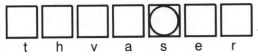 `c e l e b r a t e d` at the same time of

year as it was centuries ago.

2. A long time ago, Jewish people believed that the year ended with the gathering of the

☐ ☐ ☐ ☐ ◯ ☐ ☐ .
t h v a s e r

3. After the gathering of the harvest, a new year ☐ ☐ ◯ ☐ ☐ .
                   g b n e a

4. The Jewish new year began around the ☐ ◯ ☐ ☐ ☐ ☐ of September
                   d e m d l i

or October.

5. The first couple of High Holy Days are

☐ ☐ ☐ ☐   ☐ ☐ ☐ ☐ ◯ ☐ ☐ .
o h R s   s h h H a n a a

6. During the High Holy Days, Jewish people think about their

☐ ☐ ☐ ☐ ☐ ☐ ☐ ☐ ◯ ☐ in the past year.
d w o r i n n g s o g

7. The last day of the High Holy Days is ☐ ☐ ☐ ◯ ☐ ☐ ☐ ☐ .
              o Y m p r u K i p

8. The Jewish new year celebration begins at ☐ ☐ ◯ ☐ ☐ ☐ with a
              d u n s w o n

family meal.

9. People think about being more ☐☐☐☐◯☐☐☐☐.
   h t l o h f u g u t

10. A ram's horn called a ☐☐◯☐☐☐ is sounded in synagogues at the
    f r s a o h
    beginning of the first new year service.

11. On *Yom Kippur,* many Jews ◯☐☐☐ from sunset to sunset.
    s a t f

12. A special dish made out of sweet potatoes, prunes, meat, and carrots is called
    ◯☐☐☐☐☐☐.
    m t m s e i s

13. Jewish people exchange greeting cards to ☐☐☐◯ each other a happy new year.
    i h s w

14. Jewish people believe in the Book of ☐☐☐◯.
    f i e L

15. People want God to see a ◯☐☐☐ of good deeds when He opens the Book of Life
    r y a e
    and reads their names.

16. During the High Holy Days, Jewish people try to correct any bad ☐◯☐☐☐.
    e s d e d

17. Jews dip bread called ☐◯☐☐☐☐ into honey while saying a blessing for
    l h a h a l
    a sweet new year.

18. The Jewish High Holy Days is a time when people think about the past and hope for a better
    ☐☐☐☐◯☐.
    e u r u f t

Rosh Hashanah means:

b
— — — — — — — — —   — —   — — —
1   2   3   4   5   6   7   8   9   10 11 12 13 14

— — — —
15 16 17 18

Oktoberfest

The German people have always loved the outdoors. Their calendar is filled with open-air celebrations. The most colorful of these celebrations is Oktoberfest, which begins in September and lasts sixteen days. It always ends on the first Sunday in October.

Oktoberfest dates back to 1810, when the king of Bavaria gave his people a special holiday to celebrate his son's marriage. That first Oktoberfest included a great public festival and a horse race. The following year, the Bavarians celebrated again. This time they added a farm exhibit. German festivals have always been occasions for introducing new ideas and products. Later, Oktoberfest came to include shooting contests, all sorts of other competitions, and a grand opening parade.

Gradually, Oktoberfest spread to other parts of Germany. It even came to American cities where many German immigrants lived. But Oktoberfest is still at its most beautiful in the capital city of Bavaria where it began in 1810. Thousands of visitors gather in Munich's *Theresienwiese* (a large park) to enjoy one of the finest folk festivals in Europe.

It opens with a colorful pageant of traditional costumes from Germany and neighboring countries. The Child of Munich comes next. Dressed as a little hooded monk, the Child of Munich is the symbol of the city. Then come the marching bands playing spirited music while horse-drawn wagons from Bavarian breweries roll by.

Oktoberfest is a time for eating, too. Vendors set up small street stalls and do a brisk business in foamy beer and white sausage. Among other festival favorites are beef barbecued over open pits, caraway buns, and all kinds of pastries and other sweets. Nobody leaves Oktoberfest hungry!

Oktoberfest is an opportunity to dress up in traditional costumes. Men and boys wear short leather breeches (*lederhosen*), fancy embroidered suspenders, woolen knee socks, and pointed felt Tyrolean hats. The women put on flowered *dirndle* skirts (puffed out by several layers of petticoats) and white peasant blouses with laced bodices (vests).

During the holiday, Germans perform the old folk dances that have been popular in their land for generations. At the same time, they flock to roller coasters, carousels, and flying boats. Oktoberfest is a happy combination of the old and the new.

Oktoberfest

Circle the letter next to the word or phrase that best completes each sentence. Then put the circled letters on the numbered blanks at the bottom of the page. Make sure that you put each letter on the correct blank — the one with the same number as the sentence.
When you're finished, you'll find a holiday rhyme.

1. Oktoberfest began when the king's son was to be
   K. killed   U. married   N. crowned king

2. Oktoberfest started in
   T. Bavaria   N. Bohemia   L. Bulgaria

3. The first Oktoberfest included a
   P. barbecue   R. farm exhibit   B. horse race

4. In old Germany, people were often introduced to new ideas at
   F. weddings   E. festivals   V. parades

5. Oktoberfest is celebrated in
   L. October   K. September   O. September and October

6. Munich's Oktoberfest is held
   K. at *Theresienwiese*   U. outside the city   W. indoors

7. The Child of Munich is dressed
   R. as a monk   E. in *lederhosen*   C. in national costume

8. Oktoberfest lasts for
   G. two weeks   R. six days   O. sixteen days

9. Through most of the year, the people of Munich dress in
   T. *lederhosen*   G. *dirndle* skirts   F. modern clothing

10. During Oktoberfest, the people of Munich dress in costumes designed
    M. especially for the festival   N. hundreds of years ago   D. by Tyrolean tailors

Oktoberfest has just begun.
It's time to have

___ ___ ___ ___ ___ ___ ___   ___ ___ ___!
 8   6   2   5   3   4   7   9   1   10

Christopher Columbus

Christopher Columbus was born in the year 1451 in Genoa, Italy. As a young boy he loved to watch the large sailing ships enter Genoa's harbor. Christopher's father wanted his son to become a weaver like himself. But it soon became clear that Christopher was in love with ships and the sea. When Christopher asked for permission to work on a ship, his father agreed. Soon Columbus learned how to make maps and sail ships.

As he grew older, Columbus became curious about the world beyond the harbor of Genoa. Sailors told him stories about other lands. Christopher often wondered whether the world was flat and if the ocean was full of gigantic sea monsters. More than anything, young Columbus yearned to travel to the Far East. He tried to find a country that would pay for his voyage, but all refused.

In 1486, Columbus met King Ferdinand and Queen Isabella of Spain. He asked them for help so that he could buy ships and supplies for a trip to the Far East. He tried hard to convince the king and queen that Spain would gain land and riches in gold and spices. It took six years, but Ferdinand and Isabella finally granted Columbus his wish to sail to the Indies. They promised him that he would receive ten percent of the wealth he discovered and that he would be named "Admiral of All the Oceans and Seas."

Proud and happy, Columbus set sail in 1492 in command of three ships: the Niña, the Pinta, and the Santa Maria. But he never reached the East Indies. Instead, Columbus landed on the West Indies, a group of islands south of the United States. The first place he landed in the New World was San Salvador. He called the natives of the island "Indians" because he was convinced that he had reached one of the islands off the coast of India. The natives believed that Columbus and his men were god-like creatures who came from the bellies of giant sea birds.

Columbus made three other voyages to the Western Hemisphere. On his later trips he landed at Hispaniola, an island now divided into the Republic of Haiti and the Dominican Republic. While it's true that Columbus discovered America, he never did set foot on the land that would one day become the United States.

And Columbus never did bring back the riches he had promised Ferdinand and Isabella. Spain was very unhappy with Columbus, and he died two years after his last voyage a poor and disappointed man. He never knew that because of his discoveries Spain would build a great empire in the New World. And he died too soon to understand how his voyages would lead other explorers to sail all the way around the world, visiting the places he had dreamed of as a boy but never reached as a man.

Name_____

Christopher Columbus

The statements below are either true or false. Put a "T" on the blank following every true statement and an "F" on the blank following every false statement.
   Then shade in every part of the jigsaw puzzle picture in which you see the number of a true statement. Since the first sentence is true, for example, you should shade each piece of the picture that contains the number "1."
   When you're finished, you'll see the picture that was hidden in the puzzle.

1. Columbus was born in 1451. __T__

2. Columbus was born in 1450. _____

3. Columbus was expected to do the same kind of work his uncle did. _____

4. The father of Columbus was a weaver. _____

5. Columbus first learned about ships from reading books. _____

6. When Columbus was young, he worked on ships. _____

7. Columbus gained his father's permission to be come a soldier. _____

8. Columbus wanted to learn about Genoa. _____

9. Columbus made maps as a youth. _____

10. Columbus always wanted to know more about the world. _____

11. It took Columbus half an hour to convince the king and queen of Spain to give him money for his voyage. _____

12. Columbus wanted to travel to the Far East and the Indies. _____

13. Columbus told the king that Spain would gain no land or other riches. _____

14. Columbus made six voyages to the New World. _____

15. With the permission of King Ferdinand and Queen Isabella, Columbus sailed for the Indies in 1492. _____

16. Columbus convinced the king and queen that he would find land, gold, and spices in his travels. _____

17. Columbus was named "Admiral of the Indian Ocean." _____

18. Columbus commanded the Piña, Rinta, and the Santa José. _____

19. For his trip to the Indies, Columbus was supposed to earn the title "Admiral of All the Oceans and Seas." _____

20. Columbus was to receive ten percent of all the riches he discovered in his travels. _____

21. Columbus made four voyages to the Western Hemisphere. _____

22. Columbus sailed all the way to India. _____

23. The first place Columbus landed was Florida. _____

24. Columbus returned to Spain loaded down with spices from the New World. _____

25. The Indians believed that Columbus and his men came from the bellies of giant sea birds. _____

26. The first place Columbus landed was San Salvador. _____

27. Columbus never actually set foot on the land that later became the United States. _____

28. Spain didn't care that Columbus returned without riches. _____

29. Columbus died a rich man. _____

30. On other voyages, Columbus landed in Haiti and the Dominican Republic. _____

31. Columbus knew exactly what his discoveries would mean to the future of the world. _____

32. Spain was the only country that agreed to help Columbus. _____

33. Columbus never reached the East Indies. _____

34. Columbus lived for ten years after his last voyage. _____

35. Columbus visited all the places he had dreamed of as a boy. _____

Name_____

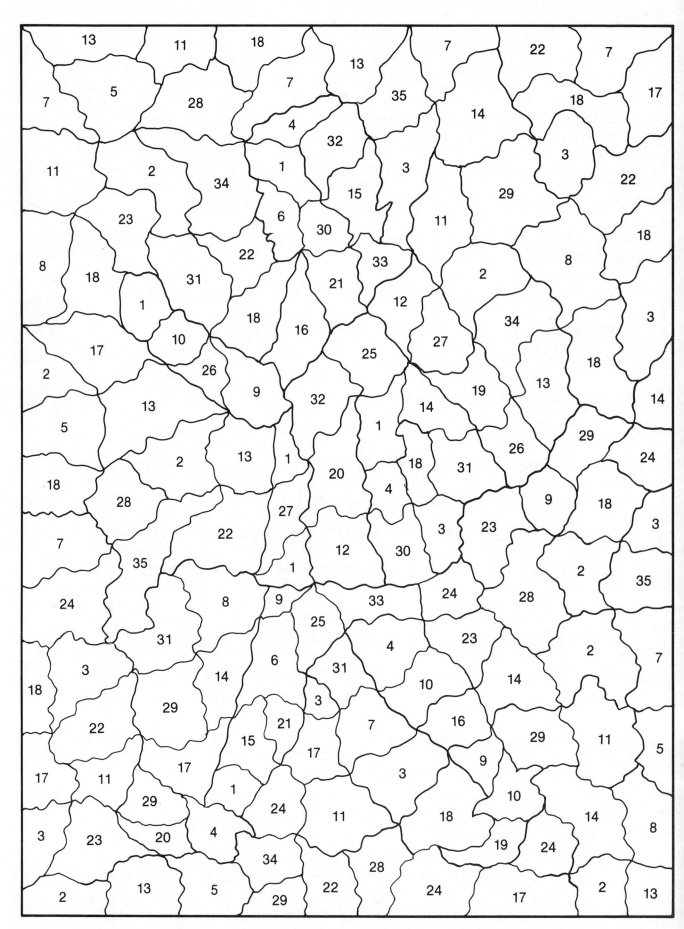

Columbus Day Celebrations

The first celebration to honor Christopher Columbus took place in Barcelona, Spain in 1493. Following his voyage across the Atlantic and back again, Columbus rode on a beautiful white horse at the head of a parade. Beside him rode King Ferdinand. The crew of the Niña and a few Indians Columbus had brought back to Spain were also in the parade.

Because he failed to bring back gold and spices, however, there were no parades after Columbus' second, third, or fourth voyages. In fact, nearly three hundred years went by before another big celebration of Columbus' discovery of America took place. On October 12, 1792, both New York and Maryland held Columbus Day celebrations.

One hundred years later, New York erected a statue to honor the explorer in Central Park's Columbus Circle. That same year, 1892, there was supposed to be a huge 400th anniversary celebration in Chicago, Illinois. Unfortunately, though, building construction of the World's Columbian Exposition wasn't completed until May 1, 1893.

Then Chicago held one of the largest parades ever. It began at 10:00 on a Wednesday morning and lasted until 2:00 in the morning on Thursday — a full sixteen hours! Thousands of people with drooping eyelids watched the parade from start to finish.

Today, Columbus Day parades are big events in many American cities. In New York City, there is a gigantic parade up Fifth Avenue, where more than 100,000 people crowd the sidewalks to watch. Meanwhile, thousands of people gather in Boston to see a wreath laid at the base of Columbus' statue. Then the Bostonians march along a traditional four-mile route.

Besides parades, there are other special events that take place on Columbus Day to honor the Italian explorer who discovered America. In Los Angeles, an Italian movie star usually participates in a flag-raising ceremony. San Francisco stages a waterfront show based on the life of Christopher Columbus. And in New Jersey, there's a pageant in which people dress up as the crews of the Niña, Pinta, and Santa Maria to re-enact the discovery of the New World. Other people dress up as Indians to greet the crews. All of these events are especially important to Americans whose ancestors came to the United States from Italy. The Columbus Day celebrations give them a chance to show pride in a fellow Italian — Christopher Columbus.

Columbus Day became a federal holiday on October 12, 1937 on the orders of President Franklin D. Roosevelt. In 1968, President Lyndon B. Johnson moved the holiday to the second Monday in October in order to create a three-day weekend. But Columbus Day isn't just an American holiday. It is now a holiday in Italy, too.

Columbus Day Celebrations

Complete the sentences below by unscrambling the letters of each missing word. Put the letters in their correct order in the boxes, and then copy the circled letters onto the blanks at the bottom of the next page. The first one is done for you.

When you're finished, you'll discover two other names for Columbus Day.

1. In 1493, Christopher Columbus rode in a [p][a][r][a][(d)][e] with King Ferdinand.
   d p r a a e

2. In 1937, [ ][ ][ ][ ][(○)][ ][ ][ ] Franklin Roosevelt set aside October 12
   i d P e t n e s r
   as a national holiday.

3. In 1892, a [(○)][ ][ ][ ][ ][ ] was erected in Columbus Circle in New York's
   t e a s t u
   Central Park.

4. Problems with building [ ][ ][ ][ ][ ][ ][ ][(○)][ ][ ][(○)][ ]
   u c c o t n i s o t n r
   delayed the World's Columbian Exposition until 1893.

5. Columbus Day parades are big [ ][(○)][ ][ ][ ][ ] in many cities.
   t v n s e e

6. The first two states to hold Columbus Day celebrations were
   [ ][(○)][ ] [ ][ ][ ][ ] and [ ][ ][(○)][ ][ ][ ][ ][ ] .
   N w e k r Y o   y d a r n M a l

7. [ ][ ][ ][ ][(○)] , the country where Columbus was born, also celebrates Columbus Day.
   a l y t I

Name_____

8. The very first parade to honor Columbus took place in
[ ][ ][ ][ ][ ][◯][ ][ ][ ] , Spain.
  e a c n r o a l B

9. A [ ][ ][ ][◯][ ][ ] in New Jersey re-enacts Columbus' landing.
  e t a n a p g

10. The 1893 Columbus Day parade in Chicago lasted [ ][ ][ ][ ][ ][ ][◯] hours.
  e i n e x s t

11. Columbus Day is a [ ][ ][◯][ ][ ][ ][ ] holiday.
  d l e a e f r

12. [ ][ ][ ] [ ][ ][ ][ ][◯][ ][ ][ ] stages a waterfront show
  a n S a i F s r c c o n
about Columbus' life.

13. The first Columbus Day celebration in America took place three
[ ][ ][◯][ ][ ][ ] years after his first voyage.
  d h u d n r e

14. In Los Angeles on Columbus Day, there is a [ ][ ][ ][◯] raising ceremony.
  g l f a

The two other names for Columbus Day are:

d __ __ __ __ __ __ __ __ day

and

__ __ __ __ __ __ __ day

West African Harvest Festivals

The tribes of western Africa live very close to nature. Every year they depend on nature to provide the right amount of sun and rain so that their crops will grow. In the United States, farmers have learned to grow more than we can eat. Even if the weather were to be dry for two or three years in a row, Americans would still have enough food. But a bad drought in western Africa means very hard times. That's why a good harvest there is an occasion for special thanksgiving.

One African tribe, the Ashanti, believes that the gods make the harvest good or bad. When the harvest is good, the Ashanti show their thanks by giving their gods things of great value. They sacrifice a sheep and offer their yam harvest, believing these gifts will please the gods and help make future harvests good. The tribe then presents the harvest to the chief. The last people to taste the yams are the men and women who worked so long and hard to harvest the crop.

Another African tribe, the Yoruba, combines the yam festival with a ceremony to honor ancestors. A few members of the tribe are chosen to be spirit-dancers. They put on long robes and masks, and then they dance through the village. These dancers represent the spirits of the dead. Because the Yoruba believe that the spirits remain on Earth to bring good or bad luck to the living, the tribe offers the yam harvest to the spirit-dancers as a gift. Knowing that the spirits have been pleased, the Yoruba people can then join in the feast.

The harvest festival of the Gā tribe is called "hunger hooting." Like the Ashanti and Yoruba, the Gā people offer gifts of food to the gods. But unlike the Ashanti and Yoruba, the Gā tribe grows corn. The hunger hooting festival involves corn left over from the year before and corn from the new harvest.

First, the Gā prepare the older corn and serve it with sacred water in their shrines. Then they eat the leftover corn to remind themselves that life is a series of harvests, season after season. Finally, they prepare, serve, and eat corn from the new harvest. As they eat, the Gā people rejoice that there is plenty, and they pray that next year will also bring a good harvest.

West African Harvest Festivals

Each of the following statements is either true or false. Decide whether a statement is true or false, and then circle the letter in the "True" or "False" column for that statement. Next, put the letter you circled on the blanks with the same number at the bottom of the page. The first statement is done for you as an example. Remember, put the circled letter on all the blanks with the same number.

When you're finished, you'll find a harvest rhyme at the bottom of the page.

	True	False
1. The tribes of western Africa live close to nature.	(r)	w
2. Among the Ashanti, the harvesters are the last to taste the yams......................	s	u
3. As part of their harvest ceremony, the Ashanti sacrifice a sacred cow.	b	i
4. Ashanti people forget about their gods when the harvest is good......................	p	l
5. The Ashanti present the harvest to the youngest member of the tribe.	n	a
6. The Yoruba people do not honor their ancestors.	o	h
7. For the Yoruba tribe, yams are an important crop.	v	m
8. The hunger hooting feast is part of the yam festival.	k	e
9. The Gā tribe celebrates the corn harvest.	n	c
10. The Gā tribe offers a gift of corn from last year's harvest................................	f	g
11. Farmers in the United States cannot grow enough food for us to eat.	d	t

Harvest Rhyme:

<u> </u> <u> </u> <u>r</u> <u> </u> <u> </u> <u> </u> <u> </u> <u> </u> <u> </u> <u> </u> <u> </u> ,
3   10   1   5   3   9   2   10   5   4   4

<u> </u> <u> </u> <u> </u> <u> </u> <u> </u> <u>r</u> <u> </u> <u> </u> <u> </u> <u> </u> <u> </u> <u> </u> <u> </u> <u> </u>
11   6   8   6   5   1   7   8   2   11   2   11   5   4   4

Halloween History

Halloween began more than 2,000 years ago among the Celtic people of Britain and France. As the days became colder and darker every autumn, the Celts made up a story to explain why winter came and all the crops and flowers died.

The Celts believed in a sun god who made the crops grow. But each year the sun god was attacked and held prisoner for six months by an evil power called Samhain. Samhain — also known as the "Lord of the Dead" and as the "Prince of Darkness" — brought the cold and darkness of winter days.

On October 31, Celtic priests (called Druids) held a new year's ceremony to mark the weakening of the sun god and the triumph of Samhain. These priests wore long, flowing white robes and met on hilltops to light bonfires. Sometimes the Druids would hurl animals or prisoners into the fires to please the cruel Samhain. The fire was strong and hot like the sun, and Druids felt sure that evil spirits would fear the fire. The priests thanked the sun god for the last good harvest, and at midnight they asked Samhain to let brightness and warmth return to the Earth.

The Celtic people, meanwhile, feared the night of October 31 more than any other night of the year. They were sure that evil spirits lurked everywhere, and they started fires in their homes to keep the evil spirits from coming inside. They believed that Samhain called dead people together and turned them into other forms, especially cats. To keep Samhain happy and to keep the evil spirits away, the Celts would put on frightening costumes made of animal skins. Often this festival to honor Samhain lasted three days.

When the Romans conquered Britain and France, they added to the Celtic Samhain festival. The Romans had two festivals called Feralia and Pomona Day that gradually blended with the Samhain festival. Feralia was a festival to honor the dead. On Pomona Day, Romans would spread out apples and nuts to show their thanks for a good harvest. The Halloween custom of bobbing for apples comes from the Roman ceremonies on Pomona Day.

The Catholic Church contributed the name "Halloween" to all these traditions. November 1 is the Catholic holiday of All Saints' Day, which honors all saints who died for their faith. The night before All Saints' Day — October 31 — was called "All Hallow Eve." Eventually, this name became shortened to "Halloween."

Halloween History

The following statements are either true or false. Put a "T" on the blank following each true statement, and put an "F" on the blank following each false statement.

Now, look at the graph sheet. For every sentence you marked with a "T," place a dot on the graph sheet where the coordinate numbers for that sentence meet. For example, sentence 1 is true. It is followed by the coordinate numbers 4-2. Starting at the 0-0 point at the lower left-hand corner, count four squares across and two squares up. Place a dot at that point.

Do the same thing for each true sentence. The first three sentences are done for you. Remember that the first number in each coordinate pair tells you how many boxes *across* from zero to count. The second coordinate number tells you how many boxes *up* from zero to count. Remember, too, that only the true statements get dots on the graph sheet.

Do sentences 1 through 31 in order, connecting the dots with lines as you go. Then lift your pencil and start again with sentences 32 through 37. Do the same thing with sentences 38 through 43 and sentences 44 through 50, lifting your pencil and starting again at the end of each group.

When you're finished, you'll see a Halloween picture appear from the empty squares.

1. Halloween dates back more than 2,000 years. __T__ (4-2)

2. All Saints' Day honors all Romans. __F__ (5-2)

3. Halloween began with the Celtic people. __T__ (6-1)

4. Halloween started in the countries now called France and Britain. _____ (9-1)

5. Halloween started in Germany. _____ (8-3)

6. The Celts worshipped a sun god. _____ (11-2)

7. The Celts had more than one god. _____ (13-5)

8. All Saints' Day was shortened to Halloween. _____ (12-9)

9. The sun god was important to the Celts. _____ (14-8)

10. The Celts believed that the sun god made crops grow. _____ (13-12)

11. The Celts loved winter. _____ (14-5)

12. The Celts made up a story to explain why winter came. _____ (11-14)

13. The reason for the Samhain festival was the change of seasons. _____ (9-15)

14. Halloween is a new holiday. _____ (8-16)

15. The Celts were afraid of the cold and the dark. _____ (6-15)

16. The Celts didn't fully understand why winter came. _____ (7-16)

17. The Celts thought that each year Samhaim attacked their sun god. _____ (8-17)

18. The Celts thought the moon god should fight to recapture its power. _____ (10-18)

19. The Celts thought of winter as the season of death. _____ (10-17)

20. Crops, leaves, and flowers die in winter. _____ (9-16)

21. The Romans went to war with Samhain. _____ (10-15)

22. According to the Druids, Samhain ruled winter. _____ (8-15)

23. Another name for Samhain was "Lord of the Dead." _____ (6-15)

24. Another name for Samhain was "Prince of Darkness." _____ (4-14)

25. Samhain was honored on November 3. _____ (3-12)

26. November 2 is All Saints' Day. _____ (5-18)

27. The Roman holiday, Feralia, honored the dead. _____ (2-12)

28. The Celts believed that Samhain called all dead people together on the evening of October 31. _____ (1-8)

29. Druid priests asked Samhain to let the darkness rule all winter long. _____ (2-9)

30. The Celts believed that evil spirits were everywhere on October 31. _____ (2-5)

31. The Celts thought that evil spirits changed into animals. _____ (4-2)

Lift Your Pencil And Start Again

32. Samhain changed the dead into cats, according to Celtic legends. _____ (11-10)

33. Druids never held ceremonies to honor evil spirits. _____ (11-15)

34. Britain brought its holiday customs to Rome. _____ (12-11)

35. Druids held ceremonies to honor Samhain and the sun god. _____ (10-12)

36. Druid priests wore long robes and held their ceremonies on hilltops. _____ (8-10)

37. The Druid priests built fires during their ceremonies. _____ (11-10)

Lift Your Pencil And Start Again

38. The Druids believed that fire was like the sun. _____ (7-10)

39. All Saints' Day honors everyone. _____ (8-15)

40. Evil spirits liked fire. _____ (9-19)

41. The Druids thanked the sun god for the last good harvest. _____ (6-12)

42. The Druids asked Samhain to let the sun god return. _____ (4-10)

43. Samhain ruled for six months. _____ (7-10)

Lift Your Pencil And Start Again

44. The custom of bobbing for apples comes from the Roman festival called
    "Pomona Day." _____ (11-5)

45. The Celts started fires inside their homes to welcome evil spirits inside. _____ (14-16)

46. Druid ceremonies marked the beginning of a three-day festival. _____ (4-5)

47. People wore costumes of animal skins during the festival. _____ (4-3)

48. Everyone marched in a big parade during the Samhain festival. _____ (5-8)

49. People dressed in costumes so that the spirits of the dead wouldn't bother them. _____ (11-3)

50. The Druids asked Samhain to let the brightness and warmth of the sun god return to
    the Earth. _____ (11-5)

Halloween Celebrations

Today, Halloween is celebrated in the United States more than in Europe. But long before American children started trick-or-treating, people in Scotland, England, and France looked upon October 31 as a day of ghosts and goblins.

In Scotland, people paraded through fields and villages with burning torches on October 31. They thought the fire would protect them from witches and ghosts. Bonfires blazed on hilltops to scare away evil spirits, and families tried to outdo one another with the largest and brightest bonfires. When the fires burned out and the last spark disappeared, these early Scots would run away yelling that the devil would catch the slowest one.

The English marched through streets carrying lighted candles to drive away witches. The English dreaded witches. If the candles burned until midnight, people felt they were safe.

In France, a man would walk through the streets on October 31, ringing a bell and warning that spirits were coming. Lanterns placed in tall stone buildings were supposed to frighten evil spirits. But sometimes, these early French people would set a plate of hot, steaming pancakes and a cup of cider on a grave to welcome the dead.

When people from Europe came to settle in the New World, they brought their Halloween beliefs with them. To many American colonists, witches and devils seemed very real, and Halloween was not a night of fun.

As pioneers moved west, they celebrated Halloween with corn-popping parties, taffy pulls, and hay rides. Farmers called these celebrations Nut Crack or Snap Apple Night. Families huddled in front of fires to roast nuts, tell ghost stories, and play games. Sometimes, Halloween was celebrated as a harvest festival, with people gathering together to have parties.

When the Irish came to the United States, Halloween became very popular in this country. Children started playing pranks on October 31, blaming the pranks on evil goblins. Ever since, Halloween in the United States has been a night filled with creepy sounds and spooky creatures.

Halloween Celebrations

Name_____

Using the words in the panels as a guide, put each set of panels back in the right order. When you have each set placed correctly, the panels will form a complete sentence and a Halloween picture.

Snap Apple

were Nut Crack

Other names

for Halloween

Night and

Night.

To many colonists

not a night of fun.

witches and devils

in America,
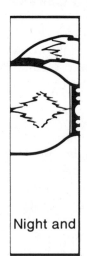

and Halloween was

seemed very real,

holiday.

Halloween became
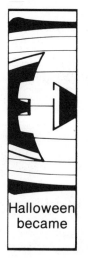

When the Irish

popular American

came to the U.S.,
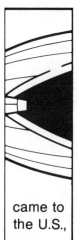

a very

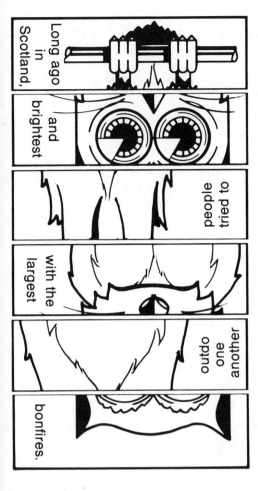

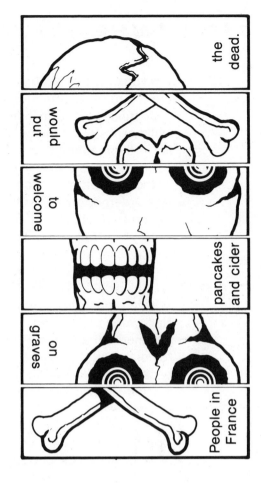

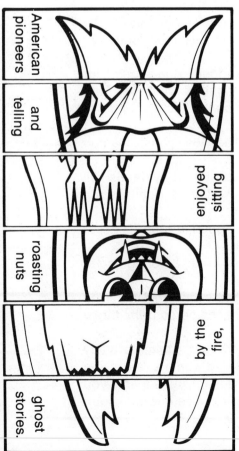

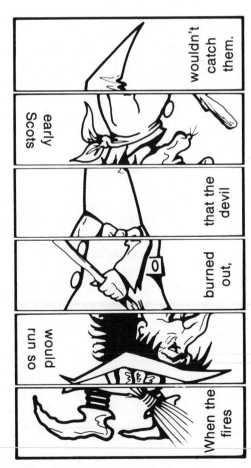

37

Halloween Customs & Superstitions

Did you ever wonder how certain customs and superstitions got started? Here are the roots of some Halloween beliefs and activities.

Costumes. A long time ago, people feared evil spirits — especially on Halloween. By putting on costumes and masks, they hoped the evil spirits would leave them alone. Sometimes, in fact, a person was chosen to dress up and —like the Pied Piper — lead the ghosts and spirits out of town.

Jack-O-Lanterns. An old Irish legend tells of a stingy man named Jack who was ordered to wander the Earth after he died, searching for a resting place. Because of all his bad deeds, Jack was forbidden to enter heaven.

When the devil gave Jack a piece of burning coal, Jack stuffed it into a turnip, making a lantern to help light his way. Irish children used to carve smiling faces on turnips. They called the carved turnips "bogies," and they carried the bogies on Halloween night to scare away witches.

When many Irish people moved to the United States, they brought their Halloween beliefs and customs with them. But instead of turnips, Irish children in America carved pumpkins. And when they put a candle inside, the Irish remembered the story of bad old Jack and the lantern. The carved pumpkin became a jack-o-lantern.

Trick-Or-Treating. Long ago in Ireland, some people celebrated "Muck Olla" on Halloween night. They would put on white robes and horsehead masks, and then march from farm to farm begging for food or money in the name of the old Druid priest, Muck Olla. In exchange for the treats, the costumed beggars offered wishes for good luck and prosperity.

In England, a custom similar to trick-or-treating was called "souling" or "soul-caking." On All Souls' Day, the poor begged for soul cakes — square buns with currents. In return for the soul cakes, the beggars promised to pray for any dead relatives of the person giving the cakes. Later, children started "souling," getting apples, buns, and sometimes money in return.

When the Irish came to the United States, tricks were added to the begging for treats. Halloween pranksters took gates off hinges, soaped windows, rang doorbells and ran away, and then blamed everything on the "little people" or "fairy folks."

Superstitions. Many Halloween superstitions started because people wanted to know what would happen to them in the future.

- Girls would throw a nut into a fire to find out whether their boyfriends still loved them. If the nut burned, their boyfriends still loved them. But if the nut burst, the boyfriends didn't care anymore.
- If a cat sat next to you on Halloween, you would have good fortune. If the cat jumped on your lap, you would enjoy fantastic luck.
- You could make a wish come true by eating a crust of bread before going to bed on Halloween night.
- A person would throw a stone into a fire to find out whether he could expect to live much longer. If the stone rolled away from the fire, the person who threw the stone would soon die.
- The Irish would cook up a dish in which they placed a ring, a thimble, a tiny doll, and a coin. If you got the ring, you would be married within a year. If you got the thimble, you'd never marry. If you found the doll in your serving, you would have children. And if you received the coin, great wealth would soon come to you.

Halloween Customs & Superstitions

Each of the statements below is either true or false. Circle the letter in the "True" column if the statement is true; circle the letter in the "False" column if the statement is false. Then put the circled letters on the blanks at the bottom of the page to spell out a hidden message. Be sure to put each letter on the numbered blank that matches the number of the sentence.

Since sentence number 1 is true, for example, you would circle the letter "a." Then you would put the letter "a" on all the blanks that have a "1" underneath.

When you're finished, you'll find the silly answer to the question: What does a witch love to eat on Halloween?

	True	False
1. The jack-o-lantern has its roots in an old Irish legend.	(a)	e
2. The French brought "little people" or "fairy folk" to the New World.	o	h
3. Bogies were turnips carved with smiling faces.	m	b
4. A long time ago, people wore costumes to keep the evil spirits away.	s	w
5. Trick-or-treating started in France.	c	n
6. Some people dressed in costumes to lead ghosts and spirits out of town.	d	f
7. On Muck Olla, businessmen marched from house to house, handing out food and money.	r	w
8. Children carried bogies on Halloween night to frighten witches away.	c	g
9. Jack placed a candle in a pumpkin when he wanted to search for a resting place.	e	o
10. "Souling" or "soul-caking" began in England.	i	a
11. Jokes and mischief on Halloween were blamed on truck drivers.	b	t
12. Muck Olla was the name of an old Druid priest.	e	o
13. Trick-or-treaters in England would receive apples, buns, and sometimes money.	l	n
14. English beggars promised to say prayers for dead relatives in return for soul-cakes.	t	y

What does a witch love to eat on Halloween?

<u>a</u> <u> </u> <u>a</u> <u> </u> <u>a</u> <u> </u> <u> </u> <u> </u> <u> </u> <u> </u> <u> </u>
 1   2   1   3   4   1   5   6   7   10   14   8   2

<u> </u> <u> </u> <u> </u> <u> </u> <u> </u> <u> </u> <u> </u> <u> </u> <u> </u> <u> </u> <u>a</u> <u> </u>
 9   5   7   2   9   13   12   7   2   12   1   11

El Dia De Los Muertos

Imagine a holiday when the dead return to their homes and visit their families! This holiday — called *El Dia De Los Muertos* — takes place in Mexico on November 1 and 2, at the same time as All Saints' Day and All Souls' Day. All Saints' Day (which honors all the saints in heaven) and All Souls' Day (a day of prayer for the souls of the dead) are solemn occasions. *El Dia De Los Muertos* is a more playful holiday.

Bakeries and toy stores start preparing for the holiday in the middle of October. Bakeries sell sweet bread shaped like human skulls and bones; it's called *pan de los muertos* (bread of the dead). They also have chocolate ghosts, skeleton candies, and *calaveras. Calaveras* are made of white sugar covered with frosting and tinsel, and they're made to look like small skulls.

Toy stores and street vendors sell toy skeletons with movable legs and toy coffins with toy skeletons inside. When someone opens the coffin, the skeleton pops out! The stores and vendors also sell special jewelry. One of the favorites is a tie pin that looks like a skeleton with dangling ribs and a ghastly grin on its face.

Families start preparing days before the holiday actually begins. In each house, they set up an altar with pictures of relatives who have died. They stock the house full of food for the returning ghosts; otherwise, the ghosts might get angry and play tricks. Among the favorite foods left on the altar are baked pumpkin, sweet bread, and sugar-candy bones.

Once the holiday starts, firecrackers explode in the night sky to light the way for the dead. Families carry a meal to the cemetery where their loved ones are buried, and they decorate the graves with orange or yellow marigolds and with flickering candles. They burn incense as they pray.

After the prayers, children play games and sing songs. Everyone enjoys plenty of food and drink, and they hope that the dead are happy, too.

El Dia De Los Muertos is a Mexican holiday, but it's also celebrated in parts of the United States where many Mexican-Americans live. Los Angeles, California, for example, celebrates the holiday with cultural displays, art shows, and street fairs. Some bakeries in the city sell *pan de los muertos,* and large papier mache skeletons hang along the parade route.

El Dia De Los Muertos is both a happy and a solemn holiday for the Mexican people. They accept death and remember their loved ones with affection.

El Dia De Los Muertos

Can you figure out what the Spanish words *"El Dia De Los Muertos"* mean? To find the answer, unscramble the letters of each missing word below. Write the letters of each word in the boxes, and then copy the circled letters in order on the lines at the bottom of the next page. The first missing word is done for you.

1. On the ┌─┐┌─┐┌─┐┌─┐⦿ **f i r s (t)** and second days of November, Mexico celebrates
   s   t   r   f   i
   El Dia De Los Muertos.

2. All Saints' Day ⦿□□□□□ saints.
       o r h n o s

3. *El Dia De Los Muertos* is a holiday in Mexico and in parts of the □□□□⦿□
                                     i e U d n t
   □□□□□□ .
   S s t   t e a

4. On □□□ □□□□□□ ⦿□□ , people offer prayers for the
     l A l   l u s S o   a y D
   souls of the dead.

5. On this holiday, the □□⦿□ return to their homes and visit their families.
               e d d a

6. Returning ghosts expect to find a house full of food; otherwise, they may get angry and
   □□□⦿ tricks.
   l y a p

7. *El Dia De Los Muertos* is also a popular holiday in Los Angeles,
   □□□□⦿□□□
   a i o i C a n l f r

8. Stores sell toy 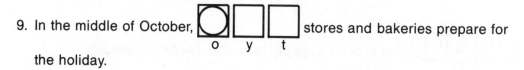 with skeletons inside
   n i c o f s f
   that pop out.

9. In the middle of October, 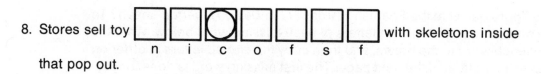 stores and bakeries prepare for
   o y t
   the holiday.

10. Bakeries sell sweet bread in the shape of  skulls and bones.
    u n h a m

11. Small skulls made of white sugar and covered with frosting and tinsel are called

    e a a r l v s c a .

12. Orange or yellow [ ] flowers are laid on graves.
    o r d m g l i a

13. [ ] explode in the sky to light the
    k c e a e s c f i r r r

    way for the dead.

14. On November 2, families visit cemeteries and bring a [ ].
    e l m a

15. *El Dia De Los Muertos* is a happy and a solemn [ ].
    l d y a o i h

The words "El Dia De Los Muertos" mean

$\underline{t}$ __ __   __ __ __   __ __
 1   2   3   4   5   6   7   8

 __ __ __   __ __ __ __
 9 10 11   12 13 14 15

Diwali

If you ever go to India during the *Diwali* Festival in late October or early November, you'll see thousands of tiny, twinkling lamps and the flash of fireworks exploding against the night sky. *Diwali* is actually a series of separate holidays. They have nothing in common except they come right after one another.

In preparation for *Diwali,* Hindu women adorn their living room floors and front entrances with *alpanas. Alpanas* are good luck designs which look like beautifully crafted carpets. To make an *alpana,* women sift thin streams of rice powder through their fingers. With the powder (which is like flour), they can create birds, flowers, or intricate patterns. Sometimes the women mix the powder with dry pigment, but often they draw in white powder and fill in with colored powders.

Schools close the day before *Diwali* so that children can make *dipas. Dipas* are oil-burning lamps that send out a warm, glowing light. They are easy to make. Children put wicks into tiny clay saucers, pour in mustard oil, and light the wicks. Then they set the *dipas* along balconies, window ledges, rooftops, and on the sides of garden paths. As many as a thousand *dipas* may decorate a single house! In many large cities, though, people are replacing the oil-burning lamps with strings of multicolored electric lights.

The people of India tell stories about the *dipa* lamps. One story involves an ancient king named Dasrath, his son Rama, and Dasrath's evil second wife. Dasrath granted his wife a wish because she had once saved his life, and the evil woman demanded that the king send Rama away for fourteen years. During Rama's absence, she plotted to have her own son made king. But at the end of fourteen years, the people of the kingdom lighted thousands of *dipas,* and Rama was able to find his way home and become the rightful king.

Dipa lamps also glow brightly to guide Lakshimi — Hindu goddess of prosperity and fortune — to people's homes. Hindus believe that if they dress in their finest clothes, scrub their houses clean, and place wreaths of flowers in the doorway, Lakshimi will come riding down on the wings of a heavenly swan to bring them prosperity for the coming year.

Diwali, like most Hindu holidays, is a time for cleansing the body. Some people bathe with perfumed oils. Others enter a river in the belief that the flowing water will wash away all evil. After cleansing themselves, the people visit temples to honor their gods.

One of the *Diwali* holidays is the business new year, called *Dhana trayodashi.* On this day, store owners settle their accounts with customers and offer prayers to Lakshimi that their businesses will prosper during the coming year.

On another *Diwali* day, families gather to honor the moon. The people of India say that the moon changes its face every fourteen days. On this *Diwali* holiday, they enjoy a special dinner of fourteen different dishes. They eat their feast in sweet-smelling living rooms, filled with incense-burning candles and lamps in the shapes of the moon.

Yama is yet another *Diwali* holiday. It is a time for brothers and sisters to make promises of love and loyalty. Boys eat a special meal with their sisters and give their sisters expensive gifts. If they don't have a sister, boys spend the day with a girl cousin.

Bali Worship Day, which is part of *Diwali,* celebrates a great Hindu battle of long ago. And still another *Diwali* day celebrates the legendary character, Vishnu. Vishnu freed the world from a monster, Naraka Chaturdashi. Children feel chills go down their spines and goose bumps all over as they listen to tales of the demon who kidnapped 16,000 beautiful maidens. Since Vishnu was triumphant, however, the holiday is a happy celebration of good winning over evil.

Diwali

Can you find your way out of the *dipa* maze? The numbers of the true statements can guide you safely from "Start" to "Out." Circle the number of each true statement, and then trace your successful route through the *dipa* maze with a pencil. But be careful! The false statements will lead you back into the maze.

1. *Diwali* takes place in May.

2. *Diwali* is made up of more than one holiday.

3. One *Diwali* holiday honors the sun.

4. Lakshimi is the goddess of love and long life.

5. *Dipa* lamps burn mustard oil.

6. *Diwali* takes place in October or November.

7. The business new year is called "Danah Charactusi."

8. Hindu people believe the moon changes its face every 14 days.

9. Schools stay open the day before *Diwali*.

10. Every home must display 1,000 *dipas*.

11. Children place mustard oil in *dipa* lamps.

12. Store owners pray to Ayodhya for luck.

13. *Dipa* lamps guide Lakshimi to people's homes.

14. Dasrath's evil wife wanted her son, Rama, to be king.

15. Store owners settle accounts with customers during *Diwali*.

16. Chaturdashi freed the world of a monster called Vishnu.

17. Some people are using strings of electric lights instead of *dipa* lamps.

18. Yama celebrates love and loyalty between brothers and sisters.

19. People scrub their houses during *Diwali*.

20. Hindus bathe during the holiday to wash away evil.

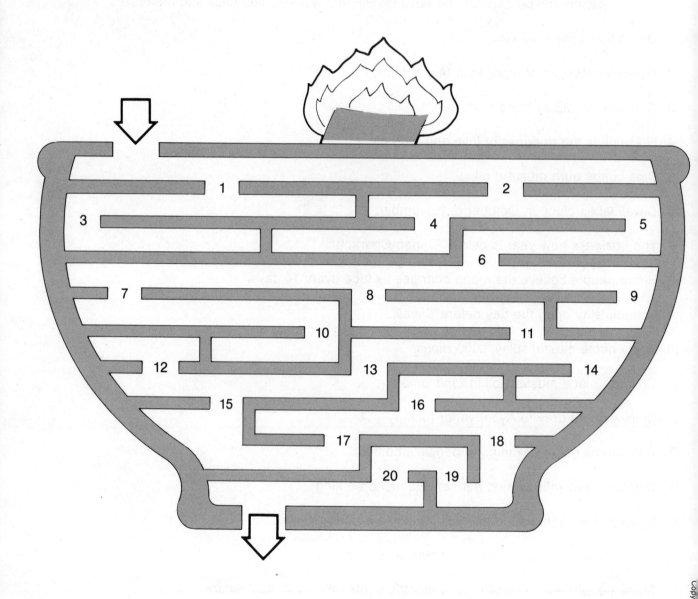

Diwali

Now it's your turn to design two *alpanas.* Dye some rice with food coloring, and then glue it down on the rectangles below. If you can't dye rice, you can decorate the rectangles with crayons, colored pencils, or felt markers.

Draw a comic strip that illustrates the story of King Dasrath, Rama, and the evil wife. Be sure to create dialogue for the characters. Put each character's words inside a cartoon balloon.

Veterans Day

The holiday we know as Veterans Day used to be called Armistice Day, and it began as a celebration of the end of World War I. When the news reached the United States that the fighting had stopped, people were overjoyed. But they didn't want to forget the many soldiers who had died to bring peace to the world. So they set aside November 11 as a day of remembrance.

The first official celebration of Armistice Day took place on November 11, 1919. Many churches held special services, and veterans who had come home from the war paraded joyfully through the streets. Most dramatic of all, people all across the United States observed two minutes of silence to honor those who had been killed during the war.

In 1921, the body of an American soldier who had been buried in France was brought to Arlington National Cemetery in Virginia. His new grave became a shrine — The Tomb of the Unknown Soldier. The inscription on the Tomb reads: "Here Rests in Honored Glory an American Soldier Known But to God." No one knew the soldier's name. He represented all the unidentified soldiers who had lost their lives in World War I. The President of the United States laid a wreath of flowers before the Tomb, and flags were lowered to half staff in respect to the Unknown Soldier.

After World War II, a second Unknown Soldier was buried at Arlington. Then in 1954, because Americans wanted to honor veterans from all wars, the name of the holiday was changed from Armistice Day to Veterans Day. Today, Veterans Day is celebrated on November 11 or on the Monday closest to that date. The President of the United States (or his representative) still lays a wreath of flowers at the Tomb of the Unknown Soldier during a special service at Arlington National Cemetery. Many cities have Veterans Day parades and programs, and flags fly from public buildings and private homes.

But the United States isn't the only country to honor men and women who served in wars. Great Britain, Canada, France, and Poland also have holidays to pay tribute to veterans.

Veterans Day

One word is missing from each of the sentences below. Write the missing word on the blanks in the flag. Then put the circled letters in order on the blanks at the bottom of the page. The first one is done for you.

When you're finished, you'll find the Canadian name for Veterans Day.

1. Armistice Day celebrated the end of _____ War I.

   W o (r) l d

2. Veterans Day falls on the 11th day of _____ .

   __ __ __ (○) __ __ __

3. Veterans Day used to be called _____ Day.

   __ (○) __ __ __ __

4. Veterans Day honors the _____ who gave their lives in wars.

   __ __ __ __ (○) __ __

5. In 1921, the Unknown Soldier was buried in Arlington National _____ .

   __ (○) __ __ __ __

6. The inscription on the Tomb of the Unknown Soldier reads: "Here Rests in Honored Glory an American Soldier Known _____ to God.

   (○) __

7. Every year, the President of the United States or his representative places a _____ on the Tomb of the Unknown Soldier.

   __ (○) __ __ __

8. Armistice Day honored all the soldiers who died during World War I to bring _____ to the world.

   __ (○) __ __

9. In 1954, Armistice Day became Veterans Day because people wanted to honor _____ from all wars.

   __ __ __ __ __ (○) __

10. During the first Armistice Day, people observed two minutes of _____ to honor the dead soldiers.

    __ __ __ (○) __

11. The first official _____ of Armistice Day took place on November 11, 1919.

    __ __ (○) __ __ __

Canadians call Veterans Day

r __ __ __ __ __ __ __ __ __ __   day
1   2   3   4   5   6   7   8   9   10 11

Shichi-Go-San

It's very lucky to be three, five, or seven years old in Japan. On November 15, the Japanese people celebrate *Shichi-Go-San,* the Seven-Five-Three Festival. This festival honors the three year olds (who are no longer babies), five year olds (who are no longer toddlers), and seven year olds (who are getting grown up).

For *Shichi-Go-San,* girls wear their best dress or a bright, colorful kimono with a long *obi* (sash) around the waist. They also wear a fancy hairpin with hanging flowers, and sometimes they put on colorful wooden sandals called *pokkuri.* Boys wear their nicest suit, or frock coat, and a bow tie.

Japanese children go with their parents to a Shinto shrine. There the parents express gratitude that their children have safely reached the age of seven, five, or three. They pray that their offspring will continue to grow up healthy and free from trouble. The Japanese show great love and respect for their children.

After visiting the shrine, Japanese families have parties for the children. Relatives and friends bring presents and money. The children gobble down a special candy called *chitoseame.* Known as the thousand-year candy, it is a hard, foot-long stick made from sugar. It tastes like a candy cane, and it symbolizes long life.

According to legend, *Shichi-Go-San* may have started long ago when Japanese parents tried to figure out why — in spite of all their love and attention — their children would sometimes cry or get angry. The parents decided that the answer must be mischief-making, squiggly little worms that entered their children's bodies. And so the parents traveled to shrines and prayed that their children might grow up without any of the trouble-making worms. They wanted their children to live good, long lives.

Today, very few Japanese families celebrate *Shichi-Go-San* the traditional way. Many years ago, the festival for three year olds was marked by the first fixing up of the children's hair. In a special ceremony called *Kamioki,* both girls and boys received a bundle of floss silk. The silk represented the white hair parents hoped their children would live long enough to have.

In the traditional festival for five year olds, boys began to wear the pleated skirts, called *hakamas,* that men wore. From this time on, boys were regarded as little men.

At the age of seven, girls were thought of as women. Until seven, girls fastened their kimono in front by tying narrow bands of cloth. But in a ceremony called *obi-toki,* the girls exchanged the cloth for an *obi,* made of hard brocaded silk. Then they attended parties and went to shrines to celebrate their new status in the family and in society.

Shichi-Go-San

Select the right word from the three choices to complete each sentence about *Shichi-Go-San*. Then put the circled letter or letters from the right word on the blanks at the bottom of the next page. Be sure to enter the circled letters in order on the blanks. The first sentence is done for you.

When you're finished, you'll find that the circled letters spell the answer to the question: What do Japanese children learn from their parents?

1. Being three, five, or seven years old is ___lucky___ for children in Japan.
   fu(n)ny   unluc(k)y   (l)ucky

2. *Shichi-Go-San* takes place in the month of _____.
   A(u)gust   N(ov)ember   Oc(t)(o)ber

3. Five year olds are no longer thought as _____.
   (a)dults   chil(d)ren   toddl(e)rs

4. Three year olds are supposed to have outgrown _____.
   their (p)arents   babyhoo(d)   toy(s)

5. When Japanese children become seven, they are _____ to grow up.
   (n)eeding   b(e)ginning   never (g)oing

6. On *Shichi-Go-San,* Japanese children wear bright, colorful _____.
   sh(o)es   paja(m)as   cloth(e)s

7. Japanese parents show a great deal of _____ toward their children.
   foo(d)   res(p)ect   (f)un

8. At _____, Japanese parents pray that their children will grow up healthy.
   shrin(e)s   (c)hurches   synago(g)ues

9. Parents also pray that their children will be free from _____.
   hap(p)iness   t(r)ouble   (w)hite hair

10. The festival may have started with a belief in mischief-making _____.
    sna(k)es   e(e)ls   worm(s)

11. Candy eaten on *Shichi-Go-San* symbolizes long _____.
    lif(e)   fin(g)ernails   frien(d)ships

12. _____ and friends come to birthday celebrations for the three, five, and seven year olds.
    Enemie(s)   Rel(a)tives   Co(w)boys

13. A special foot-long hard candy is called _____.
    rock (c)andy   cane (r)ock   c(h)itoseame

14. At the age of seven, Japanese girls tie their kimonos with an _____.
    gome(n)   *sa(n)*   *ob(i)*

15. Parents and children go to a Shinto shrine _____.
    sep(a)rately   to(g)ether   c(o)nstantly

16. Japanese parents used to wonder _____ children cried or became angry.
    w(h)y   ho(w)   wh(e)re

17. During the fifth year celebration, boys traditionally wore the *hakama,* a _____ skirt for men.
    gathere(d)   pl(e)ated   (r)uffled

18. The third year celebration was originally for _____.
    girl(s) alone   boys al(o)ne   boys and gi(r)ls

19. A special hair ceremony called _____ was celebrated long ago.
    Ka(m)ioki   *uk(a)me*   *(k)aiimo*

20. In *Kamioki,* children received _____.
    fl(o)ss silk   white fuz(z)   (s)atin

21. In *Kamioki,* a gift came in a _____.
    s(qu)are   mou(nd)   bu(n)dle

22. *Chitoseame* is known as the _____ candy.
    all-da(y)   (t)housand-year   (s)ugar-free

23. The traditional pleated skirt worn by men was called a _____.
    hakam(a)   *kama(h)a*   *haam(k)a*

24. On festival day, five year old boys became _____ men.
    (g)reat   mea(n)   (li)ttle

25. At the age of seven, girls became _____ in a ceremony called *obi-toki.*
    (c)hildren   (a)dults   wome(n)

26. Seven year old girls tied their kimonos with an *obi,* the _____ of womanhood.
    (s)ymbol   nee(d)   reaso(n)

Japanese children learn from their parents that ⎮__ __ __ __ is

__ __ __ __ __ __ than the __ __ __ and

__ __ __ __ __ __ than the __ __ __ __ __ __ __ __ __ __ .

Loy Krathong

No one knows for sure how or why *Loy Krathong* began. Yet this November festival has been a favorite holiday in Thailand for more than 600 years.

Some people say that *Loy Krathong* is a holiday to pay respect to the spirits of rivers. It is a time for the people of Thailand to ask forgiveness of the goddess of water for having dirtied the rivers and canals throughout the year. But *Loy Krathong* may have started as a holiday to worship Buddha, who left his footprints on the bank of the river Nammanda.

Whatever the origins of the holiday, its meaning today can be found right in its name. *"Loy"* means "to float," and *"krathong"* means "leaf." During the festival, children fashion banana leaves into little floating *krathongs* to send down a river. First, they cut and shape the banana leaves, fastening the seams with sharp bamboo pins. Many *krathongs* look like cups, although they come in all shapes and sizes.

Next, the children decorate the sides of their *krathongs* with colorful flowers. Then they place a candle, a coin, and incense sticks inside. Finally, when all the *krathongs* are ready, the children light the candles and launch their tiny vessels to float down the river.

Each child watches his or her own *krathong* eagerly. According to legend, if the light from the candle lasts until the *krathong* disappears, the child's wish will come true.

On the night of the festival, the rivers of Thailand sparkle and shimmer. People huddle together along the river banks, laughing, smiling, and talking while dazzling fireworks explode overhead. Everyone is happy as they watch thousands of golden lights glittering on the water. It is a good night for the rivers and the people of Thailand.

Loy Krathong

Each statement below is either true or false. Circle the number of each true statement, and then shade in each box in the grid that has the same number. When you're finished, you'll see a secret message that will tell you the name of another holiday that is similar to *Loy Krathong.*

1. *Loy Krathong* is celebrated in Thailand.

2. *Krathongs* float on rivers.

3. People celebrate *Loy Kathrong* so that they can cleanse their souls with water.

4. *Loy Krathong* takes place in November.

5. People put photographs of Buddha inside *krathongs.*

6. *"Krathong"* means "leaf."

7. On festival night, rivers in Thailand are full of bright lights.

8. The word *"loy"* means "to sink."

9. *Krathongs* are made from logs.

10. On *Loy Krathong,* people ask forgiveness from the goddess of water.

11. *Loy Krathong* has been celebrated for 2,000 years.

12. One reason for *Loy Krathong* may be the worship of Buddha, who left his footprints on the bank of the Nammanda River.

13. The sides of a *krathong* are left undecorated.

14. If a child can see light from a *krathong* until it disappears on the river, a wish will come true.

15. People in Thailand keep their rivers and canals clean all year long.

16. Children place candles, coins, and incense sticks on the outsides of their *krathongs.*

5	11	16	15	8	5	8	5	16	15	11	5	15	5	8	13	16	8	3	8	16	13
14	1	1	2	10	9	8	16	8	9	3	8	9	3	16	9	8	9	1	15	13	8
15	4	4	7	10	16	5	9	11	5	16	9	16	9	11	16	5	13	4	16	11	3
5	2	3	8	1	8	9	13	16	13	9	3	11	8	15	9	3	9	6	11	15	9
3	12	13	13	6	9	13	9	5	9	16	8	5	9	5	13	5	16	7	15	13	8
8	6	8	3	14	8	7	11	2	3	15	5	1	13	8	9	1	8	1	5	2	3
16	10	16	9	10	16	15	16	14	11	16	9	10	16	1	2	7	9	12	13	15	11
8	7	8	3	4	8	1	8	4	8	9	16	6	5	6	9	12	16	14	3	1	5
15	14	16	15	2	13	10	5	6	16	15	11	2	3	12	11	14	11	7	16	4	9
11	12	13	5	1	15	4	3	10	13	9	3	6	8	7	13	10	8	10	9	7	13
8	7	9	9	6	11	12	16	1	5	1	5	4	9	14	3	4	3	6	16	12	3
5	10	16	8	12	9	2	8	6	8	12	9	1	15	1	5	7	5	4	9	1	11
9	2	3	13	1	5	6	9	7	11	2	16	7	11	10	13	2	15	14	3	10	15
15	10	16	15	1	3	14	3	12	9	10	5	10	9	7	16	6	3	7	9	6	13
16	1	11	16	6	9	10	11	14	5	14	8	4	5	2	15	12	9	12	11	14	11
13	14	9	3	14	8	7	5	10	3	10	3	12	16	6	9	10	16	2	16	7	9
15	7	10	14	10	11	12	9	7	14	1	7	14	8	12	4	1	8	10	9	1	3
12	14	14	10	12	15	10	8	4	7	6	10	2	5	14	7	4	16	6	13	4	15
16	16	3	8	15	3	15	3	9	16	5	16	11	13	5	3	12	9	5	15	5	11

Thanksgiving History

The story of America's Thanksgiving begins with the Pilgrims. Early in the seventeenth century, the Pilgrims left England in search of religious freedom. In 1608, they sailed to Holland. Then, in 1620, the Pilgrims set sail once again. Hoping to find a better life in the New World, the Pilgrims crossed the Atlantic aboard a leaky ship called the *Mayflower*.

After sailing for many weeks, the Pilgrims landed at a place we now call Massachusetts. They set up a colony at Plymouth, where they planted the seeds they had brought from England. But the seeds didn't grow well, and there was so little food for the Pilgrims that many of them starved to death.

Luckily for the Pilgrims, some nearby Indians came to the rescue. The Indians —especially one named Squanto — taught the Pilgrims how to grow native food such as corn. The Indians gave the Pilgrims more seed, and even helped build houses for the newcomers. Without help from the Indians, the Pilgrims would not have survived.

After the first harvest, the governor of Plymouth Colony — William Bradford —suggested that the Pilgrims hold a feast of thanksgiving. He felt that it was a good time to thank God for the Pilgrims' survival in their new homeland. And to their thanksgiving feast the Pilgrims invited the Indians. The Pilgrims were grateful to the Indians for helping Plymouth Colony survive. In addition, the Pilgrims hoped that the celebration would strengthen their friendship with the Indians.

No one knows the date of the first Thanksgiving feast, or even if it was called Thanksgiving. But we do know that the Pilgrims and Indians enjoyed a huge feast of deer, goose, duck, oysters, eel, bread, fruit, and corn meal pudding. The Indians brought the deer. The Pilgrims hunted for wild birds and picked wild strawberries, squash, and pumpkin for the feast. Everything was cooked over open fires, and the Indians even showed the Pilgrims how to roast corn over the flames to make popcorn! The first Thanksgiving in the New World may have lasted as long as three days.

In 1789, George Washington declared that Thanksgiving would be a national celebration. But later the holiday faded in importance. In 1827, Sarah Hale started a campaign to have Americans observe Thanksgiving once again. Her efforts were finally successful in 1863, when President Lincoln declared that Thanksgiving would be celebrated every year on the third Thursday of November. In 1941, while Franklin Roosevelt was president, Thanksgiving was moved to the fourth Thursday in November.

Thanksgiving History

Unscramble the letters to find the missing word in each sentence below. But beware! Each set of scrambled letters contains an extra letter.

   For example, in the first sentence, "i g o r s e u i l p" spells "religious" with a "p" left over. In the second sentence, the missing word is "Mayflower," and the extra letter is an "a."

   As you complete each sentence, connect the dots on the picture by drawing lines between the extra letters. Your first line would go from "p" (on the turkey's collar) to "a" (on the turkey's chest). Your next line goes from "a" to the extra letter you find in the third sentence.

   When you're finished, your picture will reveal what the modern turkey wears.

1. The Pilgrims left England for Holland because they wanted ____religious (+p)____ freedom.
   i g o r s e u i l p

2. In 1620, the Pilgrims sailed to the New World aboard the ____Mayflower (+a)____.
   a l r a f M w o y e

3. The Pilgrims landed in _____.
   t a t a M s s s s u e h t c

4. The _____ they had brought from England didn't grow well.
   e e h s d s

5. In 1827, _____ _____ campaigned to have Thanksgiving celebrated every year.
   h r a a S l w H e a

6. The first Thanksgiving was meant to strengthen the Pilgrims' _____ with the
   i s f f h r p n d e i
   Indians.

7. _____ _____ issued a proclamation which said that there would be a
   t e P d s r n s e i c i l L o n n
   Thanksgiving celebration on every third Thursday in November.

8. Governor Bradford suggested a _____ celebration after the Pilgrims' first
   g g a s T i i n v k n h r
   harvest.

9. The _____ helped the Pilgrims by teaching them how to grow corn.
   a i l n n y s d

10. The _____ of the first Thanksgiving feast is not known.
    e t a p d

Lift Your Pencil And Start Again

11. The Pilgrims were _____ for the Indians' help.
    u g m f r t a l e

12. One of the Indians was named _____.
    t q a S k n u o

13. At the first Thanksgiving, the Pilgrims enjoyed wild birds and strawberries, squash and

    _____.
    u i p p v n m k

14. The first Thanksgiving feast may have lasted for _____ days.
    e i r h e t

15. _____ was served at the first Thanksgiving.
    n P r o o d c p

16. In 1789, _____ _____ proclaimed Thanksgiving a national holiday.
    e e G g r o g W j n s n a i h t o

17. Without the help of the Indians, the Pilgrims wouldn't have _____.
    u z e s d v r i v

18. While Franklin Roosevelt was president, Thanksgiving was changed to the _____
    t o h l f u r
    Thursday in November.

19. The Pilgrims had little _____ to eat at the beginning.
    o d f o m

Thanksgiving Celebrations Through The Ages

As long as people have grown and harvested food, they have observed festivals of thanksgiving. The ancient Greeks and Romans held harvest festivals honoring their goddesses of grains and orchards. The Greek goddess was named Demeter. The Roman goddess was Ceres, whose name is the root for our word "cereal."

During these harvest festivals, people would make music and play sports and games. They would also hold a harvest parade, decorating harvest wagons with sheaves of grain. That was really the origin of the decorated floats we see in parades today. Even the choosing of a queen to ride on a parade float goes back to the time when people honored a goddess as ruler of the harvest festival.

Ever since the Middle Ages, Europeans have celebrated a harvest thanksgiving called Martinmas on November 11. The holiday is named after St. Martin of Tours, who was a fourth-century bishop credited with performing many miracles. On Martinmas, the children of Germany and the Netherlands have a parade in which they swing lanterns carved from harvest vegetables. In Switzerland, children carve designs in turnips and sing in the streets at Martinmas.

In England, the thanksgiving holiday was called Harvest Home. Farmers would give some of the harvest fruits, vegetables, and flowers to the needy. In small villages, children would write letters to neighbors who were old and poor, and then they would put the letters inside baskets of food for their neighbors. In this way, English children learned to share the bounty of the harvest season, which is the best way to express thanksgiving.

Other European harvest traditions involved the last sheaf of wheat or corn. The last sheaf symbolized the goddess of growing things. Often, it was shaped into a kern maiden or corn doll to honor the goddess. At other times, the last sheaf was made into a wreath or a bird feeder. In England, farmers saved the last sheath in the hope that its fruitfulness would pass on to the next year's harvest.

Thanksgiving Celebrations Through The Ages

Fill in the missing words in the sentences below. Then find and circle those words in the word search puzzle. The first one is done for you.

When you finish, you'll see that there are letters left over in the word search puzzle. Put those extra letters — in order — on the blanks at the bottom of the next page.

The extra letters on the blanks will spell out a secret Thanksgiving message to you from all the turkeys.

1. Thanksgiving harvest festivals have been celebrated as long as people have grown
   __f__ __o__ __o__ __d__ .

2. After a harvest, people would always hold a
   ____ ____ ____ ____ ____ ____ ____ ____ ____ ____ ____ ____ celebration.

3. Children in England learn the real meaning of thanksgiving by
   ____ ____ ____ ____ ____ ____ ____ .

4. In Europe, thanksgiving is called ____ ____ ____ ____ ____ ____ ____ ____ ____ .

5. Ancient Greeks and Romans held a festival honoring the
   ____ ____ ____ ____ ____ ____ ____ ____ ____ of ____ ____ ____ ____ ____ ____
   and ____ ____ ____ ____ ____ ____ ____ ____ .

6. On Martinmas, children in Germany and the Netherlands parade with
   ____ ____ ____ ____ ____ ____ ____ ____ carved from vegetables.

7. The word "cereal" comes from the goddess named ____ ____ ____ ____ ____ .

8. During Harvest Home, people in England give many things to the ____ ____ ____ ____ ____ .

9. Sometimes a sheaf of wheat was kept from one harvest
   ____ ____ ____ ____ ____ ____ ____ ____ to the next so that it would pass on its
   ____ ____ ____ ____ ____ ____ ____ ____ ____ ____ ____ .

10. A long time ago, people held a ____ ____ ____ ____ ____ ____ with a
    ____ ____ ____ ____ ____ ____ ____ ____ ____ ____ ____ covered with
    sheaves of grain.

11. In England, thanksgiving was celebrated as
    ____ ____ ____ ____ ____ ____ ____ ____ ____ ____ ____ .

12. The harvest's last sheaf of wheat or corn symbolized the goddess of
    ____ ____ ____ ____ ____ ____ ____ things.

13. On November 11, people in ____ ____ ____ ____ ____ ____ celebrate a traditional harvest thanksgiving.

14. Martinmas honored ____ ____.   ____ ____ ____ ____ ____ ____

____ ____   ____ ____ ____ ____ ____ .

15. Farmers shaped the last wheat or corn sheaf into a ____ ____ ____ ____

____ ____ ____ ____ ____ ____ ____ , ____ ____ ____ ____

____ ____ ____ ____ , ____ ____ ____ ____ ____ ____ ____ , or ____ ____ ____ ____

____ ____ ____ ____ ____ ____ .

h	a	r	v	e	s	t	h	o	m	e	p	a	r	a	d	e	e	a
g	r	o	w	i	n	g	t	h	a	n	k	s	g	i	v	i	n	g
o	r	c	h	a	r	d	s	t	l	f	e	s	t	i	v	a	l	o
d	m	a	r	t	i	n	m	a	s	t	s	o	c	e	r	e	s	f
d	h	b	i	r	d	f	e	e	d	e	r	a	m	n	e	e	d	y
e	c	o	r	n	d	o	l	l	w	r	e	a	t	h	d	u	r	i
s	n	g	t	h	s	h	a	r	v	e	s	t	w	a	g	o	n	a
s	h	a	r	i	n	g	n	k	k	e	r	n	m	a	i	d	e	n
e	f	o	o	d	f	r	u	i	t	f	u	l	n	e	s	s	s	g
s	t	m	a	r	t	i	n	o	f	t	o	u	r	s	i	v	i	n
g	t	l	a	n	t	e	r	n	s	i	e	u	r	o	p	e	m	e

Turkeys suggest that you...

e ____ ____   ____ ____ ____ ____   ____ ____   ____ ____ ____

____ ____ ____ ____ ____

____ ____ ____ ____ ____ ____ ____ ____ ____ ____ ____

____ ____ ____ ____

Lucia Day

The feast of *Santa Lucia* (Saint Lucy), celebrated on December 13, is a time for great festivities in Italy, Sweden, Norway, and parts of the midwestern United States.

Most of what we know about Saint Lucy comes from legend. She was probably born around the year 283 in Sicily. Her parents were wealthy Christians at a time when the Roman rulers forbade anyone to be a Christian. Lucy and her parents had to worship in secret.

Lucy was engaged to marry a pagan, but he became angry with her — perhaps because she tried to break the engagement or perhaps because she gave so much of her money to the poor. In any case, he told the Roman authorities that Lucy was a Christian, and they quickly captured her and sentenced her to die by fire. But as the flames blazed all around her, Lucy was not harmed. Finally, the Romans had to kill her with a sword.

Lucy became a popular saint. By the sixth century, Romans were celebrating her feast day on December 13. Many other Italian cities honored her by lighting bonfires and holding torchlight processions. Later, Lucy's fame spread to Sweden, where her feast day came at the same time as the winter solstice — the shortest day and darkest night of the year. Lucy, whose name in Latin (*Lux*) means "light," became a symbol of new hope.

For centuries now, the feast of Saint Lucy — or *Luciadagen* — has been an occasion for family festivities in Sweden. Every year, the eldest daughter in each Swedish home looks forward to playing the part of the *Lussibrud* (Lucia bride). At dawn, she dresses in a long white robe tied with a bright red sash. On her head she places a wreath of burning candles. She greets the other members of her family with the song "Santa Lucia" and offers them hot coffee and a special holiday treat called *lussekatter* (Lucia cats). *Lussekatter* are small twisted saffron buns, baked in the shape of an "X," with eyes made of raisins.

It is a great honor for a young lady to be chosen the Lucia bride of an entire village. She visits each home, accompanied by the children in the village. The girls also wear long white gowns with red sashes, just like the *Lussibrud,* but they carry the lighted candles instead of placing them on their heads. The boys are called *St. Järngossars* (star boys). They, too, dress in white, and they wear tall pointed silver caps.

In addition to homes and villages, other places — schools, hospitals, and offices — choose a *Lussibrud.* In fact, if you visit Sweden on December 13, a young Lucia may knock on your hotel room door to offer you a *lussekatter!* A joyful occasion all over Sweden, Lucia Day begins the Christmas season.

Lucia Day

Complete each sentence below by filling in the missing word. Then place the letters in the candles on the numbered blanks at the bottom of the next page. Be sure to match the number below the blank with the number of the sentence from which you take each "candle letter." The first one is done for you.

When you're finished, you'll have the answer to the riddle: What warning should the Lucia bride receive before putting on her crown?

1. Much of what we know about Saint Lucy comes from
   l   e   g   e   n   d .

2. In Sweden, they call the feast of St. Lucy
   _____ _____ _____ _____ _____ _____ _____ _____ .

3. Italians celebrated with bonfires and with torchlight
   _____ _____ _____ _____ _____ _____ _____ _____ _____ in Lucy's honor.

4. St. Lucy was probably born in _____ _____ _____ _____ _____ .

5. Lucy was engaged to marry a _____ _____ _____ _____ .

6. When Lucy was put in a fire, the flames did her no
   _____ _____ _____ .

7. Finally, Lucy was killed by a _____ _____ _____ _____ .

8. In Sweden, December 13 came at the time of the winter
   _____ _____ _____ _____ _____ _____ _____ _____ .

9. The person chosen as *Lussibrud* in Swedish homes is the oldest
   _____ _____ _____ _____ _____ _____ .

10. The *Lussibrud* dresses in a gown of pure _____ _____ _____ _____ _____ .

64

11. The Latin word for "Lucia" is *lux* which means

____  ____ ____ ____.

12. It is a great honor to be chosen the *Lussibrud* of an entire

____ ____ ____  ____ ____ ____.

13. The *Lussibrud* wears a crown with seven ____ ____ ____ ____ ____  ____.

14. The *Lussibrud* sings the song "Santa ____ ____ ____ ____ ."

15. A Swedish *Lussibrud* wears a red ____  ____ ____.

16. The *Lussibrud* greets her family in the morning with hot

____ ____ ____ 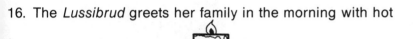 ____.

17. A special holiday treat is a

 ____ ____ ____ ____ ____ ____ ____ ____ ____.

18. On December 13, a Swedish boy may be a

____ ____. ____ ____ ____  ____ ____ ____ ____ ____.

19. *Lussibruds* are chosen by schools, offices, and

____ ____ ____ ____ ____ ____ ____ ____.

20. Lucia Day begins Sweden's Christmas ____ ____ ____ ____ ____ ____.

What warning should the Lucia bride receive before putting on her crown?

____ ____ e ____ ____ ____   ____ ____ ____ ____ ____ ____
19   12   1   15   8   20   4   14   18   2   17   16

____ ____ ____ ____   ____ ____ ____ ____!
7   11   9   10   3   5   6   13

Hanukkah History

Hanukkah is a joyous holiday for the Jewish people. Starting on the twenty-fifth day of the Hebrew month of *Kislev* (usually about the middle of December), the holiday celebrates a miracle that took place more than 2,000 years ago.

Back then, a cruel Syrian-Greek king named Antiochus ruled the Jewish homeland of Palestine. Antiochus demanded that Jews give up their religion and worship Greek gods. Any Jew who disagreed was killed. And to make sure that they would not practice their religion, Antiochus closed the Jewish temple in Jerusalem. Later, he used the temple to honor Greek gods.

There were Jews, though, who refused to obey Antiochus. One of them was Mattathias, and he fled to the hills with his five sons to escape being killed. Soon more and more Jews joined Mattathias until they had formed a small army.

At the head of the army was the son of Mattathias, Judah. Because Judah was so strong and brave, he was nicknamed Maccabee — which means "The Hammer." After many years of fighting, Judah's army defeated the forces of King Antiochus. The Jewish people returned to Jerusalem, free to worship and practice their religion as they pleased.

But first they had to cleanse the temple to make it holy once again after it had been used by Antiochus. They wanted to re-dedicate the temple to God. The word "Hanukkah" means "dedication" in Hebrew. To make the temple holy, they planned to keep an eternal light burning. But the Jews had only enough oil to keep the flame alive for one night.

Somehow, the oil burned for eight days instead of just one. And that is the miracle that Hanukkah celebrates. But Hanukkah also celebrates the determination of a people to defend their right to worship as their conscience tells them.

Hanukkah History

Each of the following statements is either true or false. Decide whether a statement is true or false, and then circle the letter in the "True" or "False" column for that statement. Next, put the circled letters in order on the blanks at the bottom of the page. The first statement is done for you as an example. When you're finished, you'll find another name for Hanukkah.

	True	False
1. Hanukkah is celebrated for nine days.	m	(f)
2. An eternal light had to burn to make the temple holy.	e	o
3. Hanukkah celebrates a war for religious freedom.	s	m
4. Jews celebrate Hanukkah in November.	f	t
5. King Antiochus wanted Jewish people to worship Greek gods.	i	e
6. Judah was the son of Maccabee.	n	v
7. Hanukkah is a time for sorrow.	o	a
8. Hanukkah celebrates a miracle that took place more than 2,000 years ago.	l	b
9. Judah's nickname was "The Wrench."	s	o
10. Hanukkah is a Hebrew word that means "devotion."	c	f
11. After they defeated the army of King Antiochus, the Jewish people re-dedicated their temple to God.	l	d
12. King Antiochus allowed Jews to worship as they pleased.	p	i
13. Jews who disagreed with King Antiochus were killed.	g	t
14. The Jews lost the Maccabean war.	r	h
15. Hanukkah takes place in the Hebrew month of *Keslow*.	n	t
16. After the Maccabean war, the Jews returned to Jerusalem	s	g

Another name for Hanukkah is

f
— — — — — — — — — — — — — — — —
1 2 3 4 5 6 7 8 9 10 11 12 13 14 15 16

Hanukkah Celebrations

Hanukkah is a happy holiday for the Jewish people, filled with songs and laughter and the flickering of candles. The holiday celebration begins at sundown. Families gather together to light the first candle of the nine-branched candlestick called a *menorah.*

The *menorah* stands for light, truth, and liberty. Every night of Hanukkah, Jews light one additional candle until all are burning. Eight of the candles represent the eight days that the light miraculously burned in the ancient temple. The ninth candle is called the *shammash;* it is the servant candle used to light all the others.

In the United States, Hanukkah is often a time for giving gifts. Some families give gifts each night of Hanukkah as another candle is lighted on the *menorah.* Children eagerly await their Hanukkah *gelt,* coins made of chocolate and wrapped in gold foil.

At Hanukkah parties, children enjoy a special food called potato *latkes* (pancakes) sprinkled with sugar or smothered in applesauce. And they play the *dreidel* game. A *dreidel* is a square spinning top stamped with the Hebrew letters *nun, gimel, hay,* and *shin.* The letters stand for the Hebrew words *"Nes gadol haya sham,"* which mean "A great miracle happened here."

According to tradition, *dreidel* playing began when King Antiochus wouldn't allow the Jews to study the Torah (the first five books of the Bible). Young Jewish boys would meet in groups to memorize the Torah. But when Antiochus' soldiers would come by, the boys would pretend to be playing a game with a spinning top — the *dreidel* — and the soldiers would not bother them.

In Israel, children do not receive presents at Hanukkah. But it is still a festive time in Israel. The country celebrates with a special relay race, starting where Mattathias and Judah began their fight against King Antiochus. During the race, runners pass a flaming torch that represents freedom. The relay race continues through thirty-five towns or more until the last runner sprints into Tel Aviv.

Tel Aviv is called the City of Lights during Hanukkah. Every light in every building and home is left on during the holiday. The president of Israel uses the relay race torch to light a gigantic *menorah.* Children march through the streets carrying lamps or candlesticks. And large *menorahs* shine brightly atop government buildings to signal the holiday.

Hanukkah Celebrations

Use these clues to fill in the crossword puzzle on the next page.

ACROSS

3. Israeli children do not receive _____ at Hanukkah.

5. Children eat potato _____ at Hanukkah parties.

7. The candleholder with nine branches is a _____.

9. The menorah stands for light, truth, and _____.

11. The *dreidel* game comes from the days when King _____ would not allow Jews to read the Torah.

12. At Hanukkah time in Israel, children march through the streets with candlesticks or _____.

13. Hanukkah is a time to feel _____.

DOWN

1. _____ is the name for chocolate coins given during Hanukkah.

2. Children play with a square spinning top called a _____ at Hanukkah parties.

4. In Israel, there is a special torch-bearing _____ race.

6. The ninth candle on the menorah, used to light the other eight, is called the _____.

8. The Israeli city of _____ _____ is called the City of Lights during Hanukkah.

10. One more _____ is lighted every night of Hanukkah.

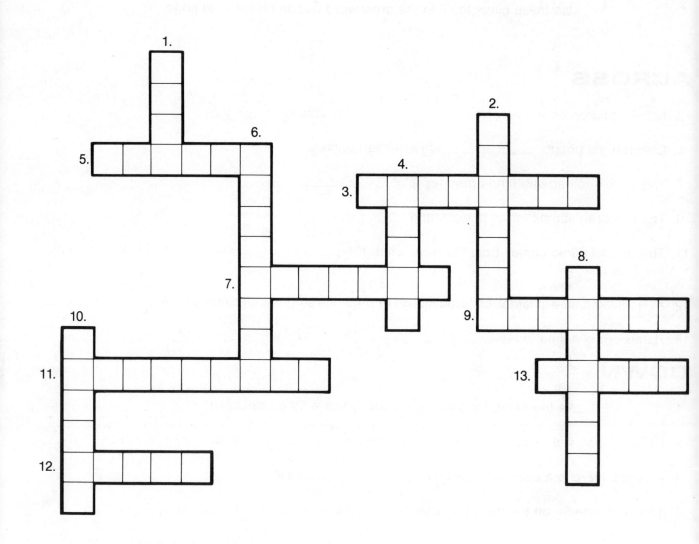

Christmas Origins

Every December, Christians all over the world look forward to the coming of Christmas. It is the most widely celebrated holiday of the year.

It started nearly two thousand years ago, with the birth of Jesus Christ. In the Bible, Saint Luke tells of an angel who appeared to the Virgin Mary. The angel told her that she would be the mother of the Savior whom God had promised His people.

Mary and her husband Joseph went to Bethlehem shortly before she was due to give birth. Because there was no room for them in the inn, they found shelter in a stable. It was there that Mary had the baby. She wrapped Him in swaddling clothes and laid Him in a manger. Then, as the angel had instructed, she named her son Jesus.

In nearby fields, shepherds were watching their flocks when angels appeared, telling them of the newborn child. The shepherds were Jesus' first visitors. Later, three wise men (known as Magi) came from the East with gifts. They found the spot where Jesus lay by following a brightly shining star.

Saint Luke never mentioned the date of Christ's birth, and there are no other records to tell us exactly when He was born. Not until the year 325 was December 25 chosen as the day to celebrate His birthday. At the same time, January 6 was selected as the day to remember the visit of the three Magi. Some Christians celebrate the Twelve Days of Christmas from December 25 to January 6.

As the centuries went by, more and more Europeans became Christians, and the Christmas holiday became more widely observed. Gradually, Christmas traditions began to include customs from many winter holidays.

Every year, many Christians travel to Israel to celebrate Christmas in Bethlehem. On Christmas Eve, they worship at the Church of the Nativity, built over the spot where it is believed the Christ Child was born. After Midnight Mass, many of the visitors walk about a mile east of the church to the Field of the Shepherds. According to tradition, this is where the shepherds lay watching their flocks when the angels appeared to them on that first Christmas night.

Christmas Origins

Fill in the blanks below to create a Christmas poem that tells the story of Christ's birth.

In the small town of ____ ____ ____ ____ ____ ____ ____ ____

A little Child was born,

Over ____ ____ ____ thousand years ago

On the first ____ ____ ____ ____ ____ ____ ____ ____ morn.

____ ____ ____ ____ wrapped Him in

____ ____ ____ ____ ____ ____ ____ ____ clothes

And laid Him in a ____ ____ ____ ____ ____ ____.

There was no room in any ____ ____ ____

For this little stranger.

In nearby fields were ____ ____ ____ ____ ____ ____ ____ ____ ____

Who watched their ____ ____ ____ ____ ____ ____ by night.

They heard the ____ ____ ____ ____ ____ ____ message

And hurried to the site.

Next came three ____ ____ ____ ____ men or Magi

Who traveled from afar.

They, too, found the Infant

By following a ____ ____ ____ ____.

Christmas Traditions

Christmas wouldn't be Christmas without its many wonderful traditions. Here's how a few of them began.

Gifts. The tradition of gift-giving is as old as Christmas itself. According to the Bible, the three Magi brought Jesus gifts of gold, frankincense, and myrrh.

Early gifts were usually homemade. Parents worked long and hard sewing rag dolls and carving wooden toys. It is still common in Germany to make a gift for the person you love best.

Santa Claus. The story of Santa Claus began with a kindly bishop named Saint Nicholas. He lived in the fourth century near Turkey, and he often passed out gifts to children and poor people in secret.

Dutch seamen carried tales of this good saint and of his great generosity back to Holland. The legend grew as people pictured Saint Nicholas in bishop's robes riding on a white horse. They said he rewarded children who learned their prayers and behaved themselves.

On the feast of Saint Nicholas, December 6, Dutch children would receive presents. When Dutch settlers came to America, they brought with them their tales of the man they called "Sinter Klaas." The English settlers changed his name to Santa Claus.

In 1822, Clement C. Moore wrote a Christmas poem for his children. Called "A Visit from Saint Nicholas," it introduced the Santa Claus with eight reindeer that we know today. In 1862, the well-known cartoonist Thomas Nast was the first to draw Santa in a fuzzy fur-trimmed suit. Through the years, Santa Claus has become fatter and jollier. In 1930, a red-nosed reindeer named Rudolph became part of the Santa Claus story.

Christmas Trees. Evergreen trees have been a part of European winter celebrations for many centuries. The trees, sometimes decorated or trimmed with candles, were thought of as symbols of everlasting life.

The custom of decorating trees for Christmas began in Germany. An eighth century monk named Saint Boniface wanted people to stop worshipping their sacred oak, so he suggested that they decorate a fir tree in honor of the Christ Child. By the 1500s, Christmas trees were very popular in Germany, and the idea was spreading to other parts of Europe.

Each country developed its own way of decorating the Christmas tree. In Poland, people attached feathers, ribbons, or colored paper to their trees. Lithuanians made little bird cages or windmills of straw for decorations. Germans were the first to make glass ornaments for Christmas trees. Just about everywhere, though, people put candles on the trees.

German settlers brought the idea of the Christmas tree to America. In the early days of this country's history, the decorations were simple: popcorn and cranberries strung and draped over paper ornaments, chains, and stars, and wax candles in simple tin holders. President Franklin Pierce set up the first Christmas tree in the White House in 1856. But it wasn't until 1895 that a telephone operator named Ralph Morris came up with the truly "bright" idea of stringing the first set of electric Christmas tree lights.

Christmas Cards. Early in the 1800s, English schoolboys would send "Christmas Pieces" to their parents, trying to show off their best writing skills. Not until around 1840, however, did the first real Christmas cards appear in England. Often, they were hand-colored. Frequently, people would compete in contests for the best card design. In one contest, the top prize was $10,000 — a great deal of money now and a fortune back in the nineteenth century!

By 1870, many people in England were sending Christmas cards, and the idea soon caught on in America. Louis Prang, a German immigrant to the United States, began printing colored cards in his Massachusetts factory in 1875. Today, Americans send millions of cards to each other every Christmas.

Carols. Music has always been an important part of Christmas. The Bible tells of the angels' song over Bethlehem on the first Christmas night. By the fifth century, Christians were writing Christmas hymns in Latin. During the Middle Ages, troupes of costumed actors traveled from village to village, presenting a Christmas story in song. Singing and traveling gradually blended into the custom of caroling.

The true Christmas carol has its roots with Saint Francis of Assisi in Italy. From Italy, carols spread to France, to Germany, to England, and to the rest of Europe. Some of the earliest Christmas carols were folk songs passed down from parent to child. Many of the songs were lullabies about the Baby Jesus.

Caroling now is popular all around the world. In some parts of Europe, carolers are known as "star singers" because they walk behind a huge star hoisted atop a pole. Children dressed as the three Magi join the procession as the carolers sing about the joys of Christmas.

Nativity Scenes. Saint Francis had the idea for the first Nativity scene. He used a live ox and donkey, and he had his students play the parts of Mary and Joseph (with a baby as Jesus) to teach his poor country parishoners the story of Christmas. Some people use the French word *crèche* for the group of traditional figures representing the first Christmas Day.

Christmas Traditions

Matched correctly, the ornament halves below form complete sentences about Christmas traditions. Each half to the left of the line has a matching half on the right side. Color matching halves the same color. Then make a Christmas tree out of green construction paper, cut out your ornaments, and paste the ornaments on the tree.

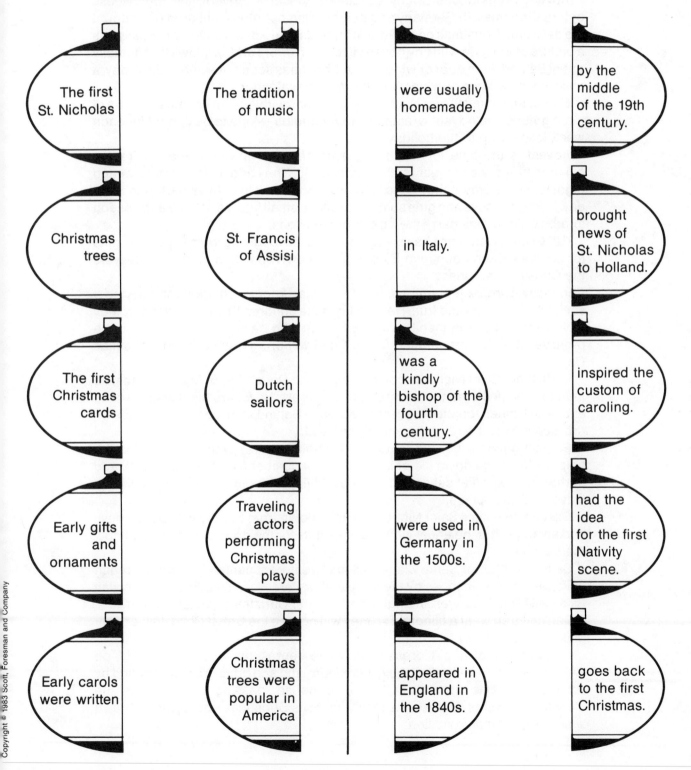

The first St. Nicholas

Christmas trees

The first Christmas cards

Early gifts and ornaments

Early carols were written

The tradition of music

St. Francis of Assisi

Dutch sailors

Traveling actors performing Christmas plays

Christmas trees were popular in America

were usually homemade.

in Italy.

was a kindly bishop of the fourth century.

were used in Germany in the 1500s.

appeared in England in the 1840s.

by the middle of the 19th century.

brought news of St. Nicholas to Holland.

inspired the custom of caroling.

had the idea for the first Nativity scene.

goes back to the first Christmas.

75

Christmas in Europe

People in Europe have many interesting Christmas customs. Some of these customs go back centuries. Although many have become popular throughout the world, a great number of others are still limited to European Christmas festivities.

Advent Preparations. Many Europeans observe Advent, the four weeks before Christmas. In Germany and neighboring countries, children often count the days until Christmas on an Advent calendar. An Advent calendar usually has a picture of a village with tiny houses filled with doors and windows that actually open! Behind each door or window is a Christmas scene or symbol. Each day, a child opens a door or window of the Advent calendar.

Europeans count the weeks before Christmas with Advent wreaths. A circle of fresh greens, the Advent wreath has four candles — one to be lighted for each week leading up to the holiday.

Advent is the time for displaying a *crèche,* or Nativity scene. In France, children prepare a manger for the Christ Child. They add a piece of straw each night for some prayer they have said or a good work they have performed that day. In Poland, boys and girls sometimes place small figures of Mary and Joseph in a box. Then they carry the box in processions.

Gift Giving. Christmas has always been a time for giving gifts, especially gifts for children. Each country in Europe has its own special person who delivers the Christmas surprises.

In many European countries, Saint Nicholas knocks on the door carrying a sack full of cookies and fruit. He questions the children to find out whether they have been good, and then he rewards those who have with treats. Finally, he promises the children that the Christ Child will bring them gifts on Christmas Day.

In Holland, Saint Nicholas comes by boat on December 6. After he lands, he mounts a white horse to ride through the streets. He wears his bishop's robes and a tall miter (pointed hat) on his head. Behind him comes Black Peter, dressed in velvet and representing the devil.

Belgian children believe that Saint Nicholas comes with a helper. It is the helper who slides down the chimney each December 6 to leave toys, gifts, and perhaps *klasses* (flat cakes with a child's initials in them) in the shoes children leave by the fireplace.

Czechoslovakia's Saint Nicholas comes down from the sky with both a devil and an angel. It is the angel who provides gifts for the good children who know their prayers.

Saint Nicholas, or Santa Claus, has many different names in Europe. French children leave their shoes by the fireplace for *Pere Noël.* Swedish children wait for a visit from *Jultomten.* In England, it's Father Christmas who brings the gifts. Italian children wear a blindfold so they will not see the Christ Child deliver their gifts.

In Switzerland, a girl dressed in white represents the Christ Child on Christmas Eve. She is called the *Christkindle,* and she rides in a sleigh pulled by six reindeer. She goes from house to house, passing out gifts. As the *Christkindle* enters a house, the family lights its Christmas tree. Germany has a similar *Christkindle* tradition.

Christmas Trees. The custom of decorating Christmas trees began in Germany, but most people throughout Europe practice the custom today. In Germany, Austria, Poland, and England, parents often decorate the tree behind tightly shut doors. The children are not allowed to see the tree until Christmas Eve. On that night, the parents throw open the doors, and the children go rushing in to see the shining tree.

Christmas Feasts. Christmas dinner is important everywhere in Europe, but each country has its own traditions. Sometimes the tradition involves a surprise. People in Denmark and Sweden, for example, hide an almond in the Christmas pudding. The lucky person who finds the almond wins a prize. Similarly, the Greeks prepare a special bread with a coin inside.

The Swedish Christmas feast includes a smorgasbord, followed by fish or ham. Yet even all that food is not enough for some young Swedes. They go from door to door asking for treats. This Swedish Christmas custom, very similar to Halloween trick-or-treating, dates back to Viking times.

Before the Christmas meal in Poland and Lithuania, families share a flat wafer that represents the love and goodwill of the season. This tradition is so strong that family members who cannot be at home on Christmas receive their parts of the wafer in the mail.

To remind themselves of the manger where Christ was born, Serbians (a group that lives in one part of Yugoslavia) cover their dining table with straw. Czechoslovakians leave one seat empty at the Christmas feast table for the Christ Child.

Christmas Sharing. Christmas is a time to remember others, and many European countries have special sharing customs.

The Irish place a candle in the window, inviting all travelers to share the warmth within the house. The candle is a way of remembering Mary and Joseph's search for lodging on that first Christmas night.

Europeans even include animals in Christmas sharing. Austrian villagers decorate a tree with bread crumbs to feed wild birds. Scandinavian children treat the birds by trimming a pole with sheaves (bundles) of wheat. In Denmark, farm animals receive loving attention at Christmas time.

One old European tradition says that farm animals gain unusual powers at midnight on Christmas Eve. Based on the belief that farm animals were in the stable when Christ was born, the tradition has it that the animals kneel at midnight in His honor. And in many parts of Europe, people believe that animals gain the power to talk at the stroke of midnight on Christmas Eve.

The day after Christmas is a special day for sharing in England. Long ago, working people collected their tips and other Christmas remembrances in earthenware boxes. Because the boxes were opened on December 26, the day after Christmas became known as "Boxing Day."

Christmas In Europe

Each picture below presents a European Christmas custom. Write a sentence for each picture, describing the custom and identifying the country where the custom is observed.

78

Christmas In Europe

Choose six European countries and enter as many Christmas facts as you can about each in the chart below.

Country	Who Brings Children Gifts? When?	What Are The Special Christmas Foods?	What Are The Special Christmas Traditions?

Christmas In Europe
Talking Animals

In Europe, many Christmas legends tell of animals — at midnight on Christmas Eve — being given the power of speech. An old French folk play has animals talking about the birth of Christ. In parts of Austria, people believe that stable animals gossip about the faults of humans who might be listening to their conversations. And a Lithuanian Christmas tale has the cattle, sheep, and horses comparing notes on how well they have been treated through the year.

Suppose that on one magical Christmas Eve you could listen in as some farm animals — or even your own pets — started talking to each other. Make up a play or story about what you might hear.

The Chimney Legend

How does Santa Claus get into houses? In European Christmas customs, he usually enters by the front door. But in many parts of the world, young children are sure he comes down the chimney.

The chimney idea may have started in a legend about the real Saint Nicholas. He was a man who always gave his gifts in secret. Once he heard about three sisters who were very poor, and so he climbed up on their roof and dropped three bags of gold down their chimney.

Can you think of another way the belief in Santa's coming down the chimney might have started? Write the legend as you imagine it, and then draw a series of pictures to illustrate your story.

Christmas In Europe

At the Christmas Eve smorgasbord in Sweden, the father dresses in a red suit, wears a white beard, and hands out the family's presents. On each package is a little rhyme that contains a clue to the gift inside. The person who gets the gift reads the rhyme aloud and tries to guess what is in the box.

Think of a gift to put inside each of the boxes below. Then write a little rhyme hinting at what each gift is. See if your friends can guess the contents of the boxes after reading your short poems.

Christmas In Latin America

On December 16, Christmas is still nine days away. But on that night, children in Mexico and Central America begin a special celebration. It is the first night of *Las Posadas.*

Las Posadas is a pageant, re-enacting Mary and Joseph's search for lodging in Bethlehem. The word *"posada"* means inn or lodging house, and the pageant is based on an old folk play brought to America by Spanish missionaries.

Some families hold the entire *Las Posadas* in their own homes. But more often, nine families get together to plan the celebration. On each of the nine evenings before Christmas, the families form a candlelight procession and march through the streets. Children usually lead the procession, carrying tiny statues of Mary and Joseph on tall sticks. Those sticks are called *andas.* Often, two children at the front of the procession are dressed as Mary and Joseph.

The procession stops at every house, and the marchers sing a song asking for shelter. Eight times they are turned away and told that there is "no room at the inn." But when they announce at the ninth house that Mary, Queen of Heaven, is seeking shelter, they are all made welcome. The marchers then place their small statues in the family's *nacimiento,* or Nativity scene.

Now it is time for *fiesta!* Each night a different family hosts the gala party. At the *fiesta* there is music, dancing, and holiday food.

For the children the best part of the *fiesta* is the *piñata.* The *piñata* is a bowl of earthenware or papier mâché made to look like a bird, a fish, a burro, or even a fat Santa Claus. The outside is often covered with brightly colored streamers. The inside is filled with sweets, toys, and other surprises — but not for long!

One by one, each child is blindfolded, handed a stick. and given three chances to hit the *piñata.* When one child finally does smash it, all the children join in a mad scramble to collect the prizes that come tumbling down to the ground.

Christmas Eve in Latin America is *Noche Buena* (the good night). On this night, the search for lodging ends at the church. Bells chime and fireworks explode to announce Christ's birth, and at midnight many attend Mass. Christmas Day itself is a religious holiday. Families gather together. They may exchange a few gifts, but they save most of their gift giving for the Epiphany (twelfth night) celebration on January 6.

Because it's warm all over Latin America in December, the Christmas feast often takes place outdoors. In Mexico, the meal begins with *ensalada de la Noche Buena,* a mixture of fruit, vegetables, and small candies. Mexicans also eat roast turkey, tortillas, and fried hot peppers. And they finish their Christmas feast with a popular dessert called *buñuelos,* made of deep-fried batter and served in a sauce of honey or powdered sugar.

Families in Central America also eat turkey at the Christmas feast. Less fortunate families, unable to afford turkey, eat stuffed tamales. The tamales are made of ground corn and filled with pieces of turkey, chicken, or pork. They may also contain raisins, olives, almonds, and chili. The stuffed tamales are wrapped in banana leaves.

In many parts of South America, a suckling pig is the center of the Christmas meal. In Brazil, the pig is served with a steamed fish pie of corn meal, cassana flour, sardines, and shrimp. In Venezuela, people enjoy *hallacas* — a sort of cornmeal pie, wrapped in plantain leaves and stuffed with pork and chicken. A favorite dessert is *dulce de lechoze,* which is green papaya and brown sugar.

But Christmas traditions in Latin America involve much more than food. Nearly everyone displays the *nacimiento,* or Nativity scene. The *nacimiento* consists of small carved or clay figures of the people in Bethlehem on the first Christmas: Mary, Joseph, the shepherds, the three Magi, and the Baby Jesus.

In Costa Rica and other Central and South American countries, an elaborate *nacimiento* fills an entire room! It is called a *presepio,* and it represents not only the manger scene but also the countryside around Bethlehem. Blue muslin creates the background for the sky and twinkling silver stars. Candles and colored lanterns illuminate the scene.

People decorate their homes with colorful flowers like the poinsettia, which is also a popular plant in the United States at Christmas. More and more families in Latin America are adding a Christmas tree to their holiday decorations.

On Christmas Eve in many Mexican villages, the local singing master leads his boys in a candlelight procession called *Pastores.* The boys carry staffs decorated with bells and tissue-paper stars. They sing joyously as they march to the local church, and they keep right on singing through the night until the dawn of Christmas Day.

At midnight on Christmas Eve in Lima, Peru, people drop to their knees in prayer. After the Midnight Mass, they sing some of the oldest Latin American carols to the accompaniment of castinets and tambourines.

In Colombia, Christmas Eve is the night of *aguinaldos* (gifts). Everyone dresses in masks and costumes and tries to guess the identity of his or her friends. Anyone who is identified must pay an *aguinaldo* to the person who guessed correctly.

Christmas In Latin America

The puzzle pieces on the following page can be arranged to form the shape of an animal. Cut out the pieces, and then see if you can shape them into a *piñata* to hang on the rope below.

As you are arranging the pieces, make sure that the words or phrases that come together along the edges of the pieces match each other. For example, the word *"nacimiento"* matches "Nativity scene." The edges of the pieces containing matching words and phrases should touch each other.

When you have solved the puzzle, paste the pieces on this paper to create a holiday *piñata*.

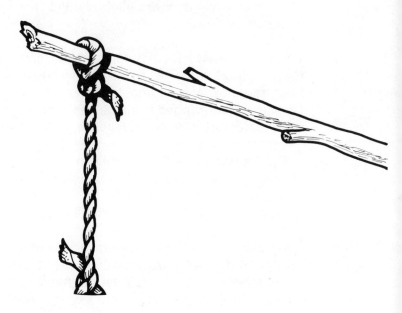

Choir Boy Procession

Las Posadas

Nativity Scene
Christmas Eve
Native To
Mexico

South
American
Dinner
Favorite

Mexican Dessert

Dulce De Lechoze

Mexico
& Central America's
Christmas Pageant

Large
Nacimiento
Nacimiento
Old Carols

Dessert Of Papayas
Pig
Noche Buena   Presepio

Pastores
Buñuelos

Poinsettia
Colombia
Peru

Night Of
Aguinaldos

Have A Merry Christmas

Below you'll find fifteen different ways to say "Merry Christmas." Each way represents a different language. You can figure out the language by unscrambling the letters in the "Language" column and writing the name correctly on the blank. The box at the bottom of the page contains all fifteen language names and should help you unscramble the letters.

Once you finish, you can start wishing your friends "Merry Christmas" in more ways than one.

	Greeting	**Language**	
1.	Feliz Navidad	nipshas	_____
2.	Glaedelig	hiasnd	_____
3.	Buone Feste Natalizie	tainali	_____
4.	God Jul Og Godt Nytt Aar	ownneriga	_____
5.	Vrolyk Kerstfeast en Gelukkig Nieus Jaar	tdhuc	_____
6.	Kellemes Karacsonyi Unnepeket	uiahnangr	_____
7.	Joyeux Noël	cnerhf	_____
8.	Froehliche Weihnachten	magnre	_____
9.	Nodlaig Mhaith Chugnat	ihris	_____
10.	Kung Hsi Hsin Nien Bing Chu Shen Tan	nicsehe	_____
11.	Houska Joulua	sifnhin	_____
12.	Boze Narodzenie	soiplh	_____
13.	Boas Festas	gurpeesotu	_____
14.	Noeliniz Ve Yeni Yiliniz Kitlu Olsum	rikutsh	_____
15.	Eem Plesierige Kerfees	narakifas	_____

Danish	**Turkish**	**Norwegian**	**Irish**	**Chinese**	**Portuguese**	**Spanish**	**French**
Afrikaans	**German**	**Hungarian**	**Italian**	**Polish**	**Finnish**	**Dutch**	

Roots of
New Year's Celebrations

The welcoming of the new year is one of the oldest holidays. It began thousands of years ago in the Near East as a springtime holiday, with people celebrating the return of warmth and growing things. The Greeks began the new year with the first full moon in June. The Egyptians held their celebrations when the Nile River flooded in July.

The modern celebration of New Year's goes back to the Romans. In the first century B.C., Emperor Julius Caesar created a new calendar that began with the month of January. The month got its name from the Roman god Janus who had two faces, one for looking backward to the old year and one for looking forward to the new year. Janus was the god of all beginnings, the god of gates and doors, and the keeper of the gates of heaven and earth. In his right hand, Janus held a key that locked the door on the old year.

During the first century, Romans greeted the new year with a party at which there was dancing, feasting, and exchanging of presents. The Romans exchanged small tree branches called *strenae,* which were supposed to bring good luck and fortune.

In the fourth century, the Romans accepted the Christian religion, and they changed their way of celebrating the new year. They thought that the beginning of the new year was a time for fasting, praying, and reflecting on past deeds. They began the practice of making resolutions to live a better life in the coming year. Under the Romans of the fourth century, New Year's became a more serious holiday.

Later, it became a noisy holiday. During the 1600s and 1700s, people made noise not only because they were having fun, but also because they were scared. They hoped that noise would frighten away the powers of darkness.

In Denmark, people banged on their friends' doors or threw cups, plates, and pottery. In Scotland, boys paraded through villages and circled houses three times while yelling — believing that their actions would scare away witches. In parts of Germany and Switzerland, boys and girls marched through the streets on New Year's Day, beating drums and kettles and blowing whistles to frighten away evil spirits.

Over the last few centuries, people have kept adding new ways to celebrate the New Year's holiday. In England, people toasted each other's health with a spiced drink called wassail, which was made of ale, sugar, nutmeg, and roasted apples. On New Year's Day, poor people and children often strolled the streets with wassail bowls, singing carols and offering New Year's greetings to all. In return, they received fruits, nuts, or money to buy wassail to fill their bowls.

Roots of
New Year's Celebrations

Use these clues to fill in the crossword puzzle on the next page.

ACROSS

3. In the fourth century, people fasted and _____ during the New Year's holiday.

5. Very long ago, people celebrated the beginning of the new year in the _____.

6. The English greeted the new year with a spiced drink called _____.

8. New Year's is one of the _____ holidays.

11. On New Year's Day in _____, people banged on their friends' doors or threw cups and plates.

13. New Year's Day was changed to January 1 when Julius Casear created a new _____.

14. In _____, boys circled houses three times while yelling in order to scare away witches.

DOWN

1. The Romans exchanged branches called _____.

2. New Year's celebrations in Rome became more serious in the _____ century.

4. People have always made _____ to live better lives in the coming year.

7. The month of January was named after _____.

9. Noise was supposed to frighten away the powers of _____.

10. Janus had two _____, one for pointing back to the old year and one for pointing ahead to the new year.

12. Romans in the first century celebrated New Year's with a _____.

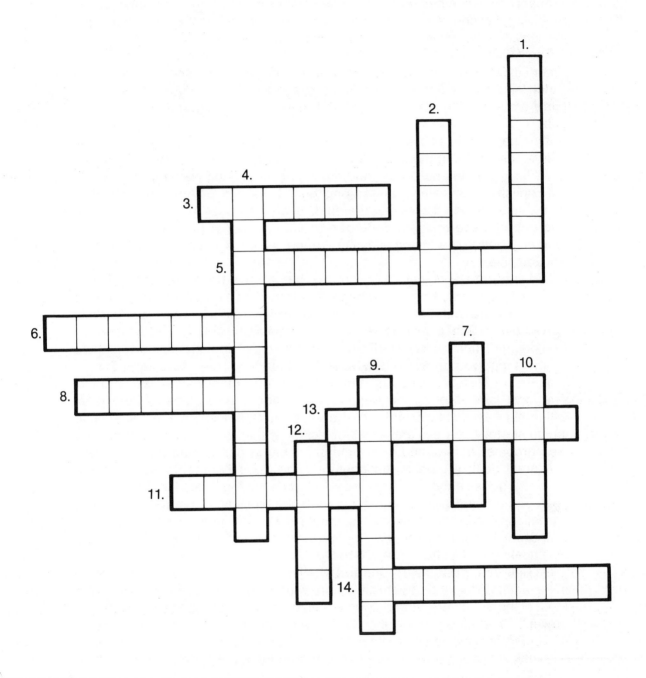

American New Year's Celebrations

Probably the first Americans to hold New Year's celebrations were the Indians. Believing that one year ended and a new one began when their corn was ripe, the Indians celebrated by wearing masks and dancing.

The Dutch were the first European settlers to celebrate New Year's in America. On New Year's Eve in New Amsterdam (later renamed New York), the Dutch families held open houses. They welcomed both friends and strangers to join them in feasting on pickled oysters, turkey, and egg nog, and in the giving of gifts.

Immigrants from all over the world who came to America brought their New Year's customs with them. Among the traditions were eating baked ham for good luck, wearing costumes, and mumming. Mumming was popular among the English and Swedish settlers along the Delaware River. As part of their New Year's celebrations, these settlers would travel from house to house in costume and put on a short play in hope of receiving money or gifts. The custom of mumming led to the Mummer's Day Parade, which is still an annual event in Philadelphia.

Midnight on December 31, of course, has always been the focus of New Year's celebrations. Most of the traditional New Year's practices are no longer observed. But people still think of midnight on New Year's Eve as a special time. They dress up in their best clothes, put on silly hats, and count down the minutes to midnight. When the clock strikes twelve, they blow furiously into noisemakers or shout loudly to greet the new year. And then they sing "Auld Lang Syne."

January 1, New Year's Day, is a time for watching football games and parades. The most famous of all the New Year's parades takes place in Pasadena, California. Pasadena welcomes the new year with the Rose Parade, a spectacle which stretches for five and a half miles! More than sixty floats, two hundred well-groomed horses, and twenty marching bands parade through Pasadena.

A great deal of preparation goes into the Rose Parade. In April, parade officials choose a theme. Then people start designing floats for the following year. Some floats are blanketed with 250,000 blossoms from roses, orchids, carnations, and other flowers. Designers may even use corn husks, straw, walnut shells, and lentil seeds to decorate their floats. It's not hard to understand why floats can cost from $30,000 to $100,000!

On New Year's Day, nearly one and a half million people jam the parade route in Pasadena. More than 130 million more watch the Rose Parade on television. Most of these viewers, though, don't realize that many of the floats run on "kid power." Children sit inside the floats, pedaling or turning cranks to create movement in some part of the float. The next time that you see a hand wave or an eye wink in one of the huge Rose Parade floats, think of the child inside working to make that movement happen.

It was a man named Charles Holder who first came up with the idea for the Rose Parade. Holder, a naturalist, suggested to members of the Valley Hunt Club in southern California that they should decorate carriages with flowers and drive through town on New Year's Day. And that's how, in 1890, the Rose Parade tradition began.

Name_____

Now the Rose Parade is too expensive for many people to participate. But everyone can afford to join Pasadena's wacky Doo-Dah Parade. It has no theme, and it's only purpose is for everyone to have plenty of crazy fun. Cars stuffed with mattresses, chicken coops, and people roll down the parade route, while Girl Scouts dressed as cookies and marshmallows perform precision drills. One year, a hundred waitresses marched in the Doo-Dah Parade, making music with pots, pans, spoons, and egg beaters!

American New Year's Celebrations

Unscramble the letters to find the missing word in each sentence below. But beware! Each set of scrambled letters contains one extra letter. For example, the answer to the first sentence is the word "Dutch," and the extra letter is "t."

Put the extra letters — in order — on the blanks at the bottom of the next page. When you're finished, you'll find that the extra letters spell another name for the Rose Parade on New Year's Day in Pasadena, California.

1. The first European settlers to celebrate New Year's Eve in America were the ___Dutch (+t)___.
   t t u h D c

2. Parts of many Rose Parade floats run on "_____ _____."
   d i o k   p e r w o

3. Some settlers believed eating ham on New Year's Day brought _____ _____.
   d o u o g   u k c l

4. Californians decorated _____ with flowers for the first Rose Parade in 1890.
   g a s c r r r a i e

5. Settlers brought New Year's customs like wearing costumes and holding _____
   g n t m i i d h
   _____ services with them to America.
   r n h c h u c

6. Today, the Mummer's Parade takes place in _____.
   e a a h a i P d i h l l p

91

7. _____ has its roots among the English and Swedish settlers along the Delaware River.
m m m u g n i M

8. Every April, Rose Parade officials must choose a _____.
e e e t m h

9. The _____ were probably the first Americans to hold New Year's celebrations.
s d I n a n n i

10. Most _____ New Year's practices are no longer observed.
r i l o t d t a n i a t

11. People who can't afford to participate in the Rose Parade can enter the _____
d o o o

_____ parade.
h a d

12. The Rose Parade stretches for _____ and a _____ miles.
v i f e   h f f l a

13. The Rose Parade was the idea of _____ _____.
r l a s e r h C   o d r H e l

14. A long time ago, people held _____ _____ on New Year's Day.
e p n o   e o s o u s h

15. During mumming, people would travel from house to house and perform short _____.
s a p s y l

16. Rose Parade floats are covered with _____.
l e s e o r w f

17. After the clock strikes _____ on New Year's Eve, people sing "Auld Lang Syne."
s t g h m d i n i

Another name for the Rose Parade is the

t   __ __ __ __ __ __ __ __ __ __ __
1   2   3   4   5   6   7   8   9   10   11   12

__ __ __ __ __
13   14   15   16   17

New Year's Celebrations Around The World

Japan. In Japan, people prepare for *Shoogatsu* on January 1 by cleaning their houses. They believe that any dirt left over from the old year will keep good fortune away in the new year. They tie all brooms with red and white paper strings because brooms left untied will, according to the custom, sweep good luck away.

The Japanese decorate the outsides of their homes with pine branches and bamboo stalks which symbolize long life and virtue. They hang rice-straw rope, called *shimenawa,* on the front and back doors to bring good luck and to keep out any lurking evil.

On New Year's Eve, people in Japan hold *boonenkai* parties to forget the old year. They eat buckwheat noodles, which they think will assure a smooth change from the old year to the new one. Close to midnight, temple bells ring 108 times to announce the new year and to cleanse the 108 human weaknesses described in the teachings of Buddha. As a result, everyone can start the new year with a clean slate.

Ecuador. New Year's in Ecuador involves the whole family. On December 31, each member of the family donates a piece of clothing — an old shirt, a pair of pants, a hat, a pair of shoes, etc. Then they stuff the clothing with straw and sew the pieces together to create an old strawman. The strawman represents the old year, the *Año Viejo.*

Someone in the family writes a last will and testament for the old strawman, listing all of the family's faults. In a midnight ceremony, they read the will and then set the strawman on fire. The family's faults are supposed to disappear with the old year.

Russia. Russia's celebration of the new year centers around parties for children. *Yolkas* (fir trees) are also part of the celebration. The trees are displayed in homes and public buildings. Under a gigantic *yolka* in Moscow, actors and actresses perform Russian fables for children.

No New Year's celebration in Russia is complete without Grandpa Frost. Grandpa Frost looks very much like Santa Claus, and he comes to parties to hand out gifts to the children and to wish them a happy new year.

Slavic Countries. On New Year's Day in Bulgaria, children visit houses in their neighborhood while carrying tree branches decorated with brightly colored paper flowers. They sing happy new year songs outside the houses. When they are invited inside, the children touch everyone with their branches. Like magic wands, the branches are supposed to bring the people good luck. Afterwards, the children receive doughnut-shaped cakes called *kolaches.*

To people in other Slavic countries, New Year's is also a time for trying to bring good luck. The Hungarians believe that they must touch a live pig on New Year's to help bring good luck.

Scotland. In Scotland, the celebration of New Year's is a gigantic holiday called *Hogmanay.* At midnight on New Year's Eve, people open their front doors to push out the old year and let in the new one. Then they watch to see who will be the "first footer" to come inside.

Scots believe that if the first person to enter is a dark-haired man, good luck will come to them. Some Scots even pay a dark-haired man to be the "first footer." But if the "first footer" is a woman, a light-haired man, an undertaker, or anyone who walks with toes pointed inward, bad luck is sure to be the result.

In small towns, Scottish children sometimes dress in sheets and sing in their neighborhoods. For their reward, they receive *Hogmanay* shortbread baked in the shape of the sun.

New Year's Celebrations Around The World

Complete the sentences below by filling in the missing word or words. Then find and circle all the missing words in the word search puzzle. Look carefully! Some of the words are spelled backwards in the puzzle.

After you've found all the words in the puzzle, you'll see that there are letters left over. Place the leftover letters — in order — on the blanks at the bottom of the next page. The extra letters will spell a special New Year's message.

1. In Japan, New Year's is called _____.

2. In Russia, New Year's centers around _____ for children.

3. People in Ecuador write a last will and _____, listing their family's faults.

4. The Japanese call a party for forgetting the old year a _____.

5. Hungarian people believe they must touch a live _____ to have good luck in the coming year.

6. In Scotland, New Year's is called _____.

7. The Japanese tie all _____ with colored strings during New Year's so they won't sweep away good luck.

8. Ecuadorians make a _____ on New Year's Eve to represent the old year.

9. Bulgarian children touch people with a small _____ _____ to bring good luck.

10. To bring good luck and chase away evil, the Japanese hang _____ ropes on doors.

11. Scots believe that if a dark-haired man is the "first _____" to enter their home on New Year's Eve, they will have good luck during the coming year.

12. Japanese people clean their houses before New Year's because they believe good _____ won't visit them if any dust is left over from the old year.

13. The whole _____ gets involved in the New Year's celebrations in Ecuador.

14. _____ bells in Japan ring 108 times to cleanse the 108 human weaknesses.

15. _____ _____ looks a great deal like Santa Claus.

i	g	r	a	n	d	p	a	f	r	o	s	t	w
i	t	t	r	e	e	b	r	a	n	c	h	e	s
s	e	s	h	y	o	u	a	n	d	s	i	s	e
t	m	h	g	v	e	r	y	b	o	m	m	t	e
r	p	o	i	d	y	i	n	t	h	o	e	a	n
a	l	o	p	a	r	t	i	e	s	o	n	m	u
w	e	g	f	a	m	i	l	y	e	r	a	e	t
m	w	a	o	r	l	d	a	h	a	b	w	n	r
a	p	t	h	o	g	m	a	n	a	y	a	t	o
n	p	s	y	n	e	w	r	e	t	o	o	f	f
y	e	u	i	a	k	n	e	n	o	o	b	a	r

A New Year's Message:

__   __ __ __ __   __ __ __   __ __ __

__ __ __ __ __ __ __ __   __ __ __ __

__ __ __ __ __   __   __ __ __ __   __ __ __

__ __ __ __ __ .

New Year's Superstitions And Resolutions

Like many other holidays, New Year's has always had its superstitions. Some people think it is bad luck to put up a calendar for the new year before January 1. Others believe that whatever you do on New Year's Day will influence what happens to you the rest of the year.

Make up a few of your own New Year's superstitions:

1. _____
_____
_____

2. _____
_____
_____

3. _____
_____
_____

New Year's has also always been a time for making resolutions. In the past, people often tried to start the new year with a clean slate. They paid all their debts, and they returned any items they had borrowed.

Today, people often make resolutions about getting rid of bad habits. They promise themselves that they will stop biting their nails or that they will start keeping their bedrooms neat or that they will lose weight.

Describe some of your own resolutions, and tell how you plan to keep them:

1. _____
_____
_____

2. _____
_____
_____

3. _____
_____
_____

4. _____
_____
_____

5. _____
_____
_____

Epiphany

The twelfth day of the Christmas season, January 6, is known as the Epiphany, Twelfth Night, or Little Christmas. In Europe and Latin America, January 6 is an important religious holiday, honoring the visit of the three Magi to the newborn baby Jesus.

Epiphany has also been a day for gifts, games, and parties. In France and Belgium, people would bake fancy cakes for parties. Inside one of the cakes was a bean, and inside another was a pea. The person finding the bean became the king of the party, while the person finding the pea became the queen. The king and queen would wear paper crowns on their heads, and everyone had to obey them.

The Greeks were superstitious about Epiphany. They burned their old shoes before Twelfth Night. The odor of the burning shoes was supposed to frighten away harmful elves. In Germany, people would smoke out houses and stables with branches blessed in the church. Then they would write the initials of the Three Kings on door beams with blessed chalk in order to bring good fortune.

Some old Epiphany customs are still followed. In Mexico, people bake a ring-shaped cake in which they hide a tiny doll for some lucky child to find. In Sweden, Epiphany marks the day to take down Christmas decorations. People hold parties to "plunder the tree." Each guest at the party receives one decoration to take home and use the following Christmas. Then all the "plundered" trees are gathered together and set afire to create a huge bonfire.

In Italy, children leave stockings for Befana to fill with gifts on January 6. The legend began many years ago. According to the story, Befana was a young girl who saw the Magi pass by but was too busy sweeping to go with them. Later, she set out to find the Christ Child, and ever since she has been wandering in search of Him. An angel told her that because she missed her chance when the Magi went by, she must fill the stockings of little children on the Eve of Epiphany. At first, Befana was angry and put ashes in the stockings. Later, she changed and began leaving presents and sweets for the good children.

A Spanish legend tells of a young water carrier who was told to watch for the Magi. He filled his shoes with hay for the Magi's camels, but then he fell asleep and missed the Magi. In the morning, however, his shoes were filled with sweets. Children in Spain still put out shoes filled with straw, and in the morning they eagerly look to see what the Magi have left them.

In Syria, people tell of a traveler who left his mule tied to a tree. While he was away, the Magi passed by. To greet them, the tree bowed down. When it straightened up again, the tree lifted the mule high into its branches. The traveler had quite a surprise when he returned for his mule! Today, Syrian children believe that the Magic Mule brings them gifts on the feast of the Epiphany.

Epiphany

You have probably heard and sung the familar song, "The Twelve Days of Christmas." Epiphany is the twelfth day. Suppose you could give your family presents on each of the twelve days of Christmas. As in the song, they would receive one of something on the first day, two of something else on the second day, and so on. Write the gifts you would give each day on the lines below.

First Day, I would give 1 _____

Second Day, I would give 2_____

Third Day, I would give 3 _____

Fourth Day, I would give 4_____

Fifth Day, I would give 5 _____

Sixth Day, I would give 6_____

Seventh Day, I would give 7 _____

Eighth Day, I would give 8_____

Ninth Day, I would give 9 _____

Tenth Day, I would give 10_____

Eleventh Day, I would give 11 _____

Twelfth Day, I would give 12_____

At the end of the twelve days of Christmas, how many gifts would you have given to your family? _____

Name_____

Epiphany

Identify the place where each Epiphany tradition listed below is practiced. Write the name of the place on the blanks. Then look at the column of letters in the stars. You'll see another name for the Magi.

1. People in this country take down Christmas decorations at parties on January 6.

2. The legend of Befana came from this country.

3. Children in this land await a Magic Mule to bring their gifts.

4. People on this continent celebrate on January 6.

5. In this country, people used to bake a bean inside a cake.

6. Here, people hide a doll inside a ring-shaped cake.

7. In this country, children fill their shoes with straw for the camels of the Magi.

Martin Luther King Day

Martin Luther King, Jr. was born on January 15, 1929. Today, several states —including Illinois, Ohio, California, and Kentucky — have made his birthday a holiday. The U.S. Congress has considered making Martin Luther King Day a federal holiday, but it has not done so yet.

On January 15, many churches and synagogues across the United States hold memorial services to honor Martin Luther King. Some schools close, while others remain open and present special cultural programs on black life in America. It is a day to remember a man who devoted his life to working for equal rights for all citizens. A civil rights leader, King led the nonviolent struggle for racial equality in the United States. He wanted all people to live together in peace as brothers and sisters.

King was born and raised in Atlanta, Georgia. His mother was a school teacher, and his father was a pastor. He grew up with a strong religious background. An excellent student, he entered college at the age of fifteen. Later, he attended a theological seminary in Pennsylvania, where he became the first black in the school's history to be elected class president. He received his doctor of philosophy degree from Boston University, where he met and married Coretta Scott.

In 1954, Martin Luther King became pastor of a church in Montgomery, Alabama. Two years later, in 1956, he helped organize a boycott of Montgomery's bus system. The policy on the buses made blacks sit at the back and forced them to give up their seats to whites. The boycott led to a change in policy on Montgomery's buses, and the successful nonviolent protest brought King to the attention of the entire country.

Although he was beaten and arrested for protesting, King continued to lead peaceful demonstrations for equal rights. His most famous march took place in Washington, D.C. in 1963. He led 200,000 followers from the Washington Monument to the Lincoln Memorial. There King delivered his "I Have A Dream" speech in which he wished for a nation where all people could live in peace and freedom. In part of his speech, King said he had a dream for his four children — that one day they would be judged not by the color of their skin but by the quality of their character.

The movement for equal rights for blacks gained new strength as a result of King's march on Washington. On July 2, 1964, President Johnson signed a civil rights bill which guaranteed equal treatment under the law for all U.S. citizens.

On April 4, 1968, an assassin shot and killed Martin Luther King. Today, other people carry on the work he began to make this country and this world a better place for all people. Through their efforts, Martin Luther King's dream lives on.

Martin Luther King Day

Use these clues to fill in the crossword puzzle on the next page.

ACROSS

1. On King's birthday, there are numerous _____ services and cultural programs throughout the United States.

7. King was raised with a _____ background.

9. Martin Luther King believed in racial _____.

11. King urged people to _____ the injustice of inequality.

12. King devoted his life to working for equal _____ for every citizen.

15. Martin Luther King was a _____ _____ leader.

16. On July 2, 1964, President _____ signed a civil rights bill.

17. At his theological seminary, King was the first black to be elected class _____.

18. King married Coretta _____.

DOWN

1. Many states have made _____ _____ _____ Day on January 15 a holiday.

2. King led many peaceful _____ and demonstrations.

3. On April 4, 1968, Martin Luther King's _____ was taken by an assassin.

4. In 1956, King led a _____ to protest racial policies on buses.

5. In 1954, King became a _____ in Alabama.

6. King entered _____ when he was fifteen.

8. King wanted all people to live together as _____ and sisters.

10. King was born in _____, Georgia.

13. King always urged a _____ struggle for racial equality.

14. King's best-known protest march took place in _____, D.C. in 1963.

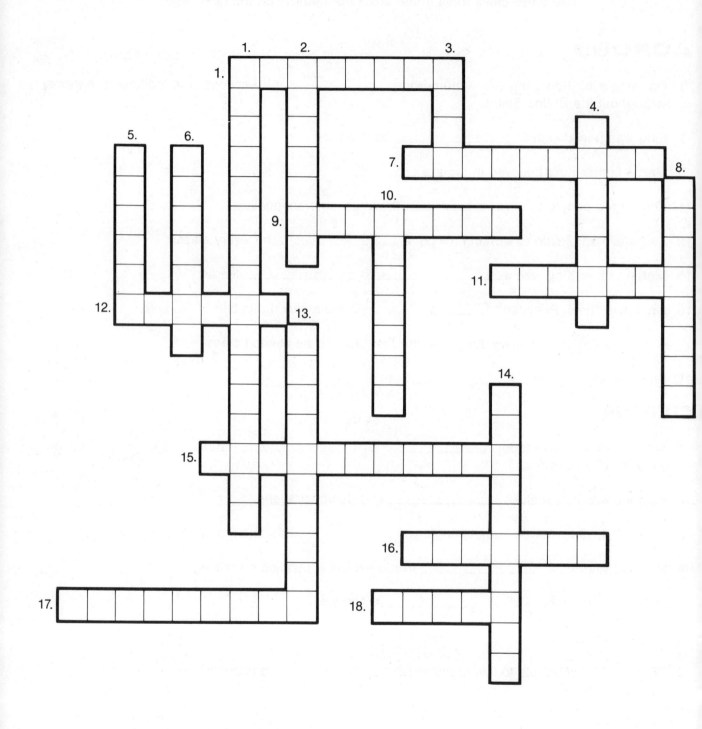

Feast Of Saint Anthony The Abbot

Dogs yelp, goats bleat, and kittens purr. It is January 17, the Feast of Saint Anthony the Abbot, and in Mexico and other parts of Latin America it is the day for the Blessing of the Animals.

Saint Anthony the Abbot was one of the earliest saints and the founder of the first monasteries. He loved both children and animals, and so it's only right that his feast day is celebrated as a holiday for children and their pets.

Churchyards throughout Latin America become bustling and noisy places. Children arrive leading dogs and cats, or carrying birds in cages, turtles in boxes, or fish in bowls and jars. Even burros, goats, sheep, and cows go to church on January 17! All the animals are carefully groomed and decorated with colorful ribbons, sparkling trinkets, and fresh flowers. Some children even dress their pets in costumes or paint bright designs on the animals with vegetable dyes.

When the local priest enters the churchyard, he blesses each animal with holy water. In the afternoon, the priest travels around the countryside to bless animals on the farms and in the pastures. No animal should be forgotten on the Feast of Saint Anthony the Abbot.

In some of the larger Latin American cities, the Blessing of the Animals occurs on a different day — often on Holy Saturday, the day before Easter. It is on this day, too, that people of Hispanic ancestry living in the United States often celebrate the Blessing of the Animals. At Our Lady of the Angels Church in Los Angeles (the oldest church in the city), the animal procession passes over the same cobblestones that Mexican settlers laid with care more than two hundred years ago.

Name_____

Feast Of Saint Anthony
The Abbot

Suppose you had the chance to have your pet blessed. How would you decorate the animal for the occasion? Describe your idea, and then draw a picture of your pet on its way to church on January 17.

Leo Politi, a famous artist who has illustrated many children's books, painted a beautiful mural showing the ceremony of the Blessing of the Animals. He painted it on a wall in downtown Los Angeles as a gift to the children of Los Angeles.

Suppose you had a chance to paint a similar mural on a wall in your city. In the space below, draw your version of children bringing their pets to church for the Blessing of the Animals.

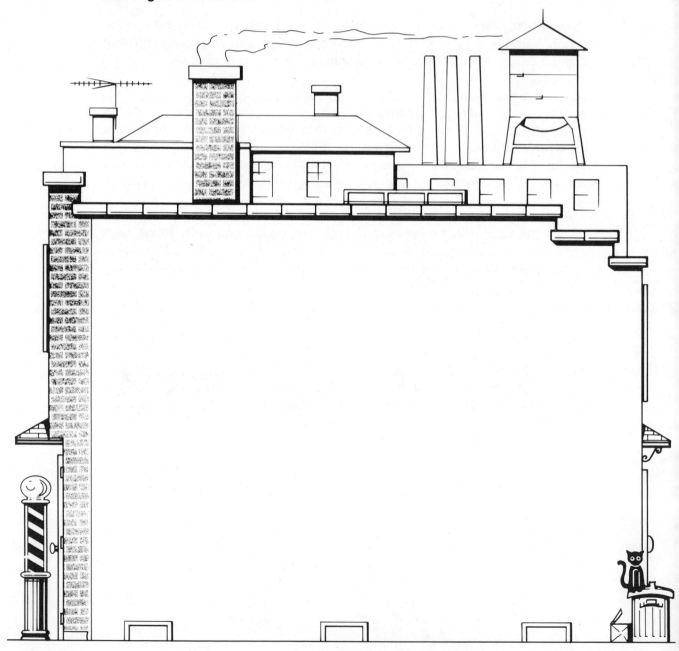

Tu B'shvat

Tu B'shvat is a springtime agricultural festival in Israel. Like Arbor Day in the United States, *Tu B'shvat* is celebrated by planting trees.

Trees are an ancient and important symbol in Jewish culture, standing for all that is good, strong, and noble in life. When a child is born in Israel, its parents plant a cedar (if it is a boy) or a cypress or pine tree (if it is a girl).

On *Tu B'shvat,* boys and girls sing as they parade up and down the streets. In their hands they carry spades, hoes, and watering cans. They may travel to an open field or find a place around their schools and homes to plant small trees. They take turns digging and collecting water for the trees.

In every village and town, people decorate their homes with beautiful flowers and fresh green leaves. Since *Tu B'shvat* is an agricultural festival, everyone eats plenty of fruit — figs, dates, raisins, and pomegranates. Long ago, people followed the custom of eating at least fifteen types of fruit on this day because the festival takes place on the fifteenth day of the Hebrew month of *shvat.*

When Israel became a nation in 1948, one of the first things people did was to plant trees. Trees created places for recreation, helped conserve the soil, provided shade from the desert sun, supplied wood for building, and allowed animals to live comfortably. Since 1948, the Israelis have planted more than 90 million trees.

Jewish families in the United States also celebrate *Tu B'shvat.* But since the holiday falls at the end of January or the beginning of February, it cannot be a springtime festival here as it is in Israel. If possible, children plant a small tree in a garden; otherwise, they may plant one in a large can indoors. Many Americans send money to Israel for the purchase of trees. Often, the trees are planted to honor someone or in memory of someone.

Tu B'shvat

Complete each sentence about *Tu B'shvat* by filling in the missing word or words. Then find those words in the word search puzzle, and shade them with your pencil.

Look carefully! The words are spelled left-to-right, top-to-bottom, bottom-to-top, even diagonally. And one of the missing words appears in the puzzle twice.

When you have shaded all of the missing words, put the letters that are both shaded and circled on the blanks at the bottom of the next page. Be sure to copy the letters in order — left to right, row by row from top to bottom. And be sure to use ONLY the circled letters that you have shaded with your pencil. If a circled letter is not part of a missing word, do not put the letter on the blanks.

If you do the puzzle correctly, you'll find that the letters you put on the blanks spell another name for *Tu B'shvat.*

1. *Tu B'shvat* is an _____ festival.

2. The festival takes place on the fifteenth day of the _____ month of *shvat.*

3. During *Tu B'shvat,* people in Israel plant _____.

4. This festival holiday dates back to _____ times.

5. It is _____ in Israel when the *Tu B'shvat* holiday is celebrated.

6. In the _____ culture, trees are an important _____.

7. Trees have always been a symbol of all that is _____, _____, and

   _____.

8. Israeli parents plant a _____ tree for a newborn boy and a _____ or pine tree for a newborn girl.

9. Israelis decorate their homes with _____ and green _____ for *Tu B'shvat.*

10. For this holiday, children travel to open _____ to plant trees or plant them near their

    homes and _____.

11. Since this is an agricultural festival, everyone eats plenty of _____.

12. Long ago, it was the _____ for people to eat at least fifteen kinds of fruit on *Tu B'shvat*

    because the holiday falls on the _____ day of the month.

13. _____ became a nation in 1948.

14. One of the reasons people planted trees in Israel was to create areas for _____.

15. Trees also provide _____ for building, help _____ the soil, give

_____ from the desert sun, and allow _____ to live comfortably.

16. Jewish families in the _____ (abbreviation) also celebrate *Tu B'shvat*.

a	s	t	r	o	n	g	c	f	s	c	h	o	o	l	s	q
m	p	g	t	r	e	c	r	e	a	t	i	o	n	a	y	v
n	r	y	x	j	r	e	j	k	c	t	w	h	u	o	m	d
o	i	r	a	r	e	g	o	o	d	e	f	r	s	z	b	l
b	n	o	b	n	m	w	m	b	y	d	d	s	e	q	o	w
l	g	f	r	d	n	f	i	e	l	d	s	a	h	v	l	s
e	t	c	y	p	r	e	s	s	i	e	o	f	r	u	i	t
t	i	s	r	a	e	l	p	t	h	g	a	l	a	d	s	m
a	m	r	e	c	r	e	a	t	i	o	n	v	o	a	l	o
n	e	f	i	f	t	e	e	n	t	h	f	o	e	r	a	t
h	e	b	r	e	w	p	i	f	l	o	w	e	r	s	m	s
o	y	g	z	a	n	c	i	e	n	t	i	t	o	c	i	u
c	o	n	s	e	r	v	e	t	r	e	e	s	m	b	n	c
s	h	a	d	e	a	g	r	i	c	u	l	t	u	r	a	l

Another name for *Tu B'shvat* is:

__ __ __ __   __ __ __ __ __ __ __   __ __ __ __ __

__ __ __   __ __ __ __ __ __ __ •

Chinese New Year

The Chinese New Year falls on the first day of the new moon (between January 21 and February 20). On this day, the Chinese give thanks for the safe and happy year just ended, and they wish each other another good year to come.

As New Year's Day approaches, great preparations begin. Families clean their homes thoroughly, especially the kitchens. They hide brooms, knives, and any sharp objects, believing it brings bad luck to use them on New Year's Day. Since only reheated food may be served during the holiday — no cooking! — women prepare food in advance for the many visitors expected.

The Chinese decorate their homes with flowers and with a "money tree." The money tree is made of pine or cypress branches from which hang old coins, fruit charms, and paper flowers. A bright red scroll hangs on the door.

On New Year's Eve, families gather for a big feast. The table is covered with a red cloth and decorated with flowers. Red candles and incense burn while people make offerings to the gods. At midnight, they lock the doors and seal them with good luck papers. Everyone wishes each other *"Bai-nien"* (Happy New Year), and younger members of the family perform a ceremonial bow called *kowtow* (which means "touch the ground with the forehead") to congratulate their elders. Everyone stays up late, believing that doing so brings longer life to parents. The family finally goes to bed when the moon reaches its highest point in the sky.

On New Year's Day, everyone dresses in his or her best clothes. It is very important, even in the poorest of families, to have new shoes to start the new year. Many attend services in the temples, and everyone speaks in a low voice.

New Year's Day is a day for giving. Friends exchange large red greeting cards. Children receive coins in small red envelopes called *li shee*. They also get gifts of oranges and tangerines.

Following an old Buddhist tradition, the family eats a lunch of special vegetables. This meal is supposed to bring good fortune through the year. After lunch, everyone visits family and friends. During the visits they eat candied melon, fruit, and *popo*. *Popo* are boiled dumplings that sometimes have a hidden surprise inside that brings the finder good luck for the new year.

Over the next few days, the New Year's celebration moves outdoors. The streets fill with holiday crowds. Children go singing from door to door, and they are rewarded with rice cakes, fruit, or sweets. Firecrackers explode, as drums and cymbals lend their beat to the Dragon and Lion Dance.

On the first full moon, the New Year's celebration ends with the great Feast of Lanterns. People carry lanterns and join in a huge parade. At the head of the parade is an enormous dragon, the Chinese symbol of strength and goodness. It is called the Golden Dragon, and it can stretch more than one hundred feet long! Carried by men and boys who prance along beneath it with only their feet showing, the Golden Dragon is made of a bamboo frame covered with silk, velvet, or paper.

According to custom, the Golden Dragon has been hibernating all year and will go to sleep again after the parade until next New Year's Day. That's why excited spectators throw firecrackers in the dragon's path — they want to make sure he stays awake!

In the United States, the biggest celebration of the Chinese New Year takes place in San Francisco, California. The festivities last nine days and include a Miss Chinatown beauty contest, a Chinese opera, folk dancing, cooking exhibits, tours of temples and Chinese businesses, and, of course, a gigantic parade.

Although the parade features many beautiful artifacts from Hong Kong, the star of the event is Gum Lung. A 120-foot Golden Dragon, Gum Lung is controlled by three relay teams of twenty-two classical dancers. The tradition of having a Golden Dragon to celebrate the Chinese New Year in San Francisco goes all the way back to 1860.

Chinese New Year

Use these clues to fill in the crossword puzzle on the next page.

ACROSS

1. There are great _____ on the Feast of Lanterns.
4. A highlight of the parade is the Golden _____.
5. Small red envelopes are called _____ *shee.*
8. New Year's _____ festivities include offerings to the gods.
10. The Golden Dragon usually has a frame made of _____.
11. On New Year's Day, the Chinese often give gifts of _____.
12. New Year's Day falls on the first day of the _____ moon.
15. It is _____ important to have new shoes for the holiday.
16. Children often receive cakes made of _____ as they go singing from door to door.
18. Boiled dumplings are called _____.
19. _____ reheated food may be served on New Year's Day.
21. _____ means "touch the ground with the forehead."

DOWN

1. Everyone takes _____ in the great parade.
2. The Chinese perform a Dragon and a Lion _____.
3. On New Year's Eve, people _____ the door with good luck papers.
6. _____ is a color used to celebrate the Chinese New Year.
7. The Chinese New Year usually falls in the month of _____.
9. On New Year's Day, children receive gifts of _____.
11. _____ wake up the sleepy dragon.
13. _____ *nien!*
14. A _____ tree decorates a Chinese home at New Year's.
17. A large _____ watches the great parade.
20. During the first day of the New Year, people keep their voices _____.

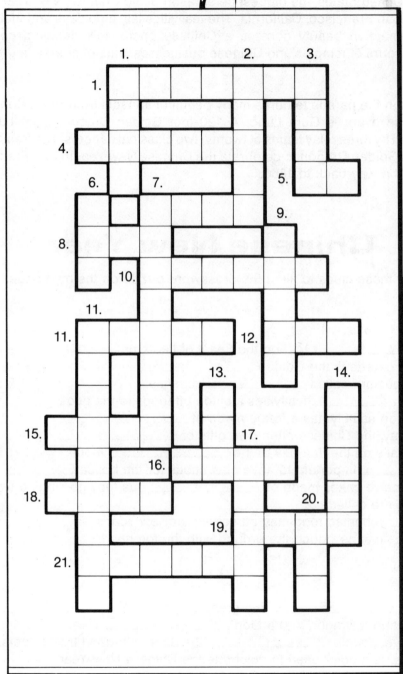

Groundhog Day

People have believed in animals as weather predictors since the Middle Ages. Farmers believed that hibernating animals would crawl out of their dens on February 2 to check on the weather.

German farmers used to watch for a badger on this day, a holiday they called *Candlemas.* When German immigrants settled in Pennsylvania, they brought their customs with them. There was one problem, though. There weren't many badgers in Pennsylvania. Instead, the Germans started to watch for a groundhog, an animal that's also known as a woodchuck.

Supposedly, what the groundhog does on February 2 is a sign of what the weather will be. If the groundhog comes out of his burrow and sees his shadow, there will be six more weeks of winter. If it is too cloudy for him to see his shadow, then farmers know that it's safe to plant their crops. No matter what he sees, of course, the groundhog always crawls sleepily back into his burrow.

Sometimes, groundhogs disagree with each other about the weather. In 1980, for example, a groundhog named Punxsutawney Phil saw his shadow in Pennsylvania. So did Jimmy the groundhog in Wisconsin. But Woodrow K. Chuck of the New York Zoo predicted an early spring when he could not see his shadow.

Most Groundhog Day celebrations in the United States take place in the East and Midwest. One of the biggest is in Punxsutawney, Pennsylvania, where the members of the Punxsutawney Groundhog Club meet every February 2 to watch for a groundhog named "His Majesty, the Punxsutawney." After they find out what the weather will be, the members gather for an interesting dinner. The menu includes such delicacies as groundhog jello, soothsayer's gravy, and forecaster's beans!

No one knows just how accurate the groundhog is as a weather predictor. Some people claim that the little animal is right at least one time out of seven.

Groundhog Day

ACROSS

1. Another name for a groundhog is a _____.
4. A groundhog is supposed to be a good weather _____.
5. If the groundhog sees its shadow, there will be _____ more weeks of winter.
8. In Germany, Groundhog Day was celebrated on _____.
9. _____ 2 is Groundhog Day.
10. As a weather predictor, the groundhog may be accurate at least one out of _____ times.

DOWN

2. Groundhogs sometimes _____ with each other's predictions.
3. Groundhog Day was first observed back in the _____   _____ .
4. One of the biggest Groundhog Day celebrations takes place in _____, Pennsylvania.
5. If the groundhog doesn't see its _____, farmers know they can plant their crops.
6. Settlers from _____ brought the Groundhog Day celebration to America.
7. German farmers used to watch for a _____ rather than a groundhog.

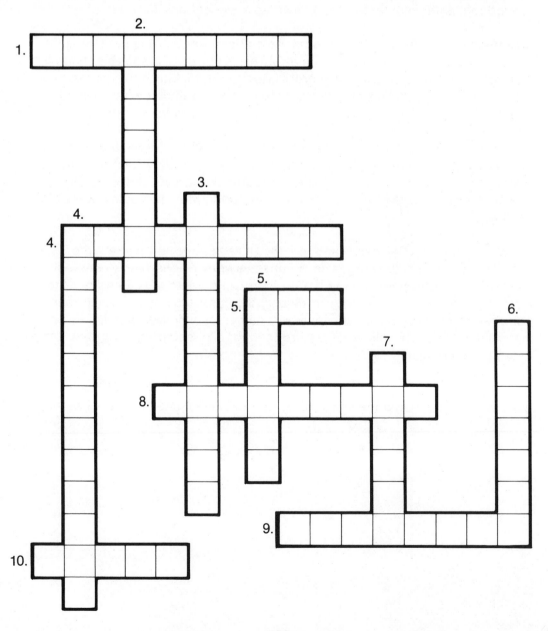

Name_____

Lincoln's Birthday

Back when Lincoln was campaigning for the presidency, he received a letter from a ten-year-old girl named Grace. Lincoln was clean-shaven at the time, and Grace suggested that he grow a beard. Lincoln not only answered Grace's letter, but also grew a beard and kept it for the rest of his life.

Now it's your turn to write a letter to the President of the United States. What suggestion(s) can you make? When you're finished with your letter, mail it to the President. You might just receive an answer.

115

Valentine's Day History

Nobody knows for certain just who St. Valentine was. As a matter of fact, church records show at least two people named St. Valentine.

Both of these men were thrown in jail. One went to jail almost 1700 years ago for performing marriages against the wishes of the Roman Emperor Claudius. Claudius forbade all marriages because he needed men for his army. Married men wanted to stay at home rather than fight with the army. St. Valentine broke the Emperor's rule by marrying those who were in love and wanted to be together.

The other Valentine was thrown in jail for helping Christians at a time when Emperor Claudius was persecuting Christians. While in jail, Valentine fell in love with the jailer's blind daughter and cured her blindness. Claudius then had Valentine beaten and beheaded. Before he died on that dark, dreary morning, he wrote a love letter to the jailer's daughter and signed it, "From your Valentine." The date was February 14.

It was in the year 496 that Pope Celasius set February 14 as the date to honor St. Valentine. The holiday fell on the day before the Roman Lupercalia festival, a time to honor the god who protected crops and animals from wolves. The Lupercalia festival was celebrated on February 15, which was almost the beginning of spring. Over the years, Valentine's Day and the Lupercalia festival were joined into one holiday, one time of celebration.

The holiday became a time to celebrate love. In addition to the St. Valentines who had been persecuted for love, the day drew its special meaning from the birds. The early Romans believed that birds chose their mates around the fourteenth of February. As a result, the Romans made that date a day for honoring human lovers, too.

One old custom involved Roman girls placing their names in a large urn. Boys would then draw the names from the urn to find out who would be their partner for one year. Church officials, however, didn't like this practice. They substituted the names of saints for the names of young women in the urn. When a boy then drew a name out, he was supposed to behave like the saint whose named he had selected. Since that wasn't much fun, the practice of using girls' names eventually came back.

When the Romans traveled through Europe, they took their customs and festivals with them. That explains how the story of St. Valentine and the holiday for lovers spread over the continent during the Middle Ages. In Italy, people would gather in gardens on February 14 to listen to love poetry and romantic music. In France, people wanting to marry were paired from lists of names read at random. Austria, Hungary, and Germany also celebrated Valentine's Day with special courtship customs.

Over the centuries, however, interest in celebrating Valentine's Day faded. In fact, the holiday might have completely disappeared had not people started to send valentine's cards. Today, millions of Americans send valentine's cards on February 14, and recently the holiday has become popular once again in many European countries.

Valentine's Day History

Each of the sentences below is either true or false. Put a "T" on the blank if the sentence is true; put an "F" on the blank if the sentence is false.

Then, with a pencil, lightly shade all the puzzle parts where you find the number of a true sentence. A hidden picture and a valentine message will soon appear. When you're finished, you can color the picture.

1. Because they came so close together, the Lupercalia festival and St. Valentine's Day were made into one holiday. _____

2. People thought that birds chose mates in the summer. _____

3. Church records show that there are at least two St. Valentines. _____

4. In the Middle Ages, people in Italy would meet in gardens on Valentine's Day to listen to love poetry and music. _____

5. Valentine's Day celebrations might have disappeared if not for the valentine card. _____

6. One St. Valentine helped people who wanted to marry. _____

7. Valentine's Day is celebrated near the beginning of fall. _____

8. Just before he died, one St. Valentine wrote a love note and signed it, "From your Valentine." _____

9. Roman girls picked boys' names from a large urn. _____

10. Pope Celasius set February 14 as the day to honor St. Valentine. _____

11. The Lupercalia festival honors the love children feel for birds. _____

12. St. Valentine was the patron of lovers. _____

13. Church records show that Pope Celasius was really St. Valentine. _____

14. One St. Valentine fell in love with a jailer's blind daughter. _____

15. The celebration of Valentine's Day never spread beyond Rome. _____

16. Roman boys picked girls' names from a large urn. _____

17. The Lupercalia festival was a time to honor the god of birds. _____

18. The Romans spread the celebration of Valentine's Day in Europe. _____

19. Valentine's Day is a very popular holiday in the United States. _____

20. Emperor Claudius forbade all marriages because he needed men for his army. _____

21. In France, people were paired for marriage from lists of names read at random. _____

22. We know exactly who the one and only St. Valentine was. _____

23. People have been celebrating St. Valentine's Day for more than two thousand years. _____

24. Church officials decided boys should draw the names of saints rather than girls. _____

25. Valentine's Day celebrations spread to Austria, Hungary, and Germany. _____

26. Today, the United States is the only country where people celebrate Valentine's Day. _____

2	22	26	9	23	22	11	17	7	22	15	7	11	2	26	23
23	9	1	11 / 2	7	3	15	12	19	24	25	9	3	8	19	15
7 / 2	26	5	17	13	6	2	9	14	11	1	7 / 18	5 / 11	4	8 / 11	26
22	7	8	15	7	10	8	16	20	8	13	25	23	12	14	13
13	26	7	9	22	13	2	15	9	17	22	23	15	2	7	1
22	1	2	4	12	14	3	6	17	1	11	1	4	6		2
23	17	18 / 5	23	10 / 11	9	19	2	12	11 / 2	10	13	10	6	18	21 / 7
9															
26	15	6	26	1	4	20	1	16	4	14	26	3	6	9	17
2	23	17	7 / 11	22	7	11	2	13	17	9	17	23	11	26	2	22

Valentine Cards & Symbols

People have been sending valentine cards to each other for hundreds of years. The oldest valentine poem and letter date back to the fifteenth century. It wasn't until the seventeenth century, however, that the custom of sending a valentine to a favorite person became truly popular.

By 1700, English boys were leaving valentine love letters on girls' doorsteps. By the middle 1700s, people were buying booklets — called "writers" — filled with valentine verses and messages. They copied the verses on gilt-edged letter paper or on sheets adorned with cupids, birds, or hearts.

It wasn't until 1800 that the first commercial valentine card appeared. Soon after that, though, the mail became crowded each February as sweethearts everywhere sent cards to one another. Frequently, the cards displayed complicated and unusual designs. Then came the novelty or comic cards. These cards featured jokes, tiny mirrors, and even slots to hold lockets of hair. While many cards cost only a penny, some of new novelty cards carried prices as high as $10!

In the early 1900s, many valentine cards were done in poor taste. As the cards lost some of their dignity, people lost their interest in sending them. Then, around 1920, valentine cards became popular once again — especially among children. Now everyone seems to be sending the February love messages once again. As a matter of fact, Valentine's Day is second only to Christmas in the number of cards sent through the U.S. mail.

Everyone loves to receive colorfully decorated cards on Valentine's Day. But do you know why the cards are red, pink, or white? And can you explain why they usually feature hearts, cupids, or birds? Here are the stories behind the symbols:

Hearts. People used to believe that the heart was the source of feelings and intelligence. Today, people speak of emotions as being stored in the heart. It's easy to understand, therefore, why the heart has always been an important symbol on Valentine's Day.

Red, White, and Pink. Love is a warm emotion, and red is the color of warmth. It is also the color of the human heart. White symbolizes purity and faith. Since pink is a blend of red and white, it stands for a blend of passion, purity, and faith.

Cupid. In Greek and Roman mythology, Cupid was the symbol of love. The Greeks called him Eros, the son of Aphrodite who was the goddess of love and beauty. In Roman mythology, his name was Cupid and his mother was Venus. Always pictured as a playful child with wings on his back, Cupid carried his bow and arrows with him everywhere. His arrows were invisible, and his targets were people's hearts. When Cupid shot a person with an arrow, the person immediately fell in love.

Doves. A long time ago, people thought birds chose mates on February 14. That belief made birds a good symbol for human love on Valentine's Day. Doves became the most popular bird symbol because of their soft cooing, their shyness, and their gentle manner.

Valentine Cards & Symbols

Complete each sentence below by writing the missing word on the blanks. Then copy the letters inside the hearts onto the blanks at the bottom of the next page. Be sure to match the number of the sentence from which you take each letter with the number under the blank at the bottom of the page. The first sentence is done for you.

When you're finished, you'll find a secret valentine message.

1. Cupid is a s y m b o l of Valentine's Day.

2. _____ _____ _____ _____ and other birds are symbols of Valentine's Day.

3. White symbolized faith and _____ _____ _____ _____ _____.

4. The Greek name for Cupid's mother is _____ _____ _____ _____ _____ _____.

5. Cupid aims his arrows at people's _____ _____ _____ _____ _____.

6. The Greeks call Cupid _____ _____ _____ _____.

7. Some novelty cards contained a tiny _____ _____ _____ _____ _____.

8. Venus is the goddess of love and _____ _____ _____ _____ _____.

9. Valentine's Day is dedicated to romantic _____ _____ _____.

10. People send cards in the _____ _____ _____ on Valentine's Day.

11. Cupid is always pictured as a _____ _____ _____ _____ child.

12. People once thought of the heart as the source of

_____ _____ _____ _____ _____ _____ _____ _____.

13. _____ _____ _____ _____ is the blend of red and white.

14. Even today, people speak of _____ _____ _____ _____ _____
being stored in the heart.

15. Cupid shoots ___ ___ ___ ___ ___ ___ ___ ___ arrows.

16. Cupid has ___ ___ ___ on his back.

17. ___ is the color that means warmth of feeling.

18. The oldest valentine poem and letter date back to the

___ ___ ___ ___ ___ ___ ___ century.

19. Valentine's Day is ___ ___ ___ ___ ___
only to Christmas in the number of cards sent through the mail.

20. The first ___ ___ ___ ___ ___ ___ ___
valentine card appeared in 1800.

21. At one time, valentine cards cost as much as ___ ___ dollars.

22. In the seventeenth century, it became the custom to send

___ ___ ___ ___ ___ ___ ___ ___ ___.

23. Booklets full of verses and messages were called valentine

___ ___ ___ ___ ___ ___.

24. Valentine ___ ___ ___ were often in poor taste in the early 1900s.

Secret Valentine Message:

y ___ ___   ___ ___ ___   ___ ___
1   2   3   4   5   6   7   8

___ ___ ___ ___ ___ ___ ___ ___ ___
9   10 11 12 13 14 15 16 17

___ ___ ___ ___ ___ ___ ___
18 19 20 21 22 23 24

Washington's Birthday

"First in war, first in peace, and first in the hearts of his countrymen." That's the way someone once described George Washington, the first President of the United States. Although Washington was born more than 250 years ago, his great deeds live on. On February 22, we remember the contributions Washington made to our country.

It was in an old red farmhouse near the green slopes of the Potomac River that George Washington was born on February 22, 1732. The son of a wealthy Virginia planter, he was the eldest of six children. George was very smart as a child, and he studied very hard. Since there were few public schools in Virginia back then, George and his friends were taught by tutors.

As a youngster, George loved horseback riding, running, and wrestling. According to legend, no one could pin George's shoulders to the ground in a wrestling match. For fun, George imagined he was head of the army. He grouped his friends into army companies under his command, and then they all marched, paraded, and fought pretend battles. Early in his life, George won respect for his truthfulness and sense of fair play.

In 1743, George's father died. George moved in with his half-brother, Lawrence, at Lawrence's home, which later became known as Mount Vernon. During his teen years, George used his great ability in mathematics to become a land surveyor. Using a compass and steel chains, he would go around measuring the boundaries of Virginia farms.

It was as a soldier rather than a surveyor, however, that George Washington first became famous. During the French and Indian War, Washington served as an officer with the British forces. He showed great courage during combat against the enemy. In 1759 he married Martha Custis, and at the end of the French and Indian War in 1763 he settled down to the relaxed life of a wealthy plantation owner.

Washington grew wheat and tobacco at his Mount Vernon plantation. For recreation, he took part in fox hunts, played with his stepchildren, and entertained his friends. As relations between England and her American colonies grew tense, though, Washington knew he must get involved. In those days, the large landowners were often the political leaders, too. Washington was elected a delegate to both the First and Second Continental Congresses.

As war broke out between England and the colonies, Congress had to pick one man to lead the American army. In 1775, it made George Washington commander-in-chief. Through all the bitter fighting of the War for Independence, it was Washington's leadership, bravery, and skill that held the American army together. Without him, the United States might not have won its victory over the British.

After the war, some Americans wanted to make Washington king of the new country, but he refused. He went back to Mount Vernon instead. In 1787, he played a leading role in the convention that wrote the U.S. Constitution. Then in 1789, he was elected the first President of the United States. He served two terms as president and refused to run for a third. During his presidency, he won respect for the new nation.

In 1797, George Washington retired once more to his home at Mount Vernon. It was there, on December 14, 1799, that he died after riding horseback on a snowy and windy day. Since his death, Washington has been honored in many ways. He is the only person since the colonial period to have a state named after him. The nation's capital bears his name, and more than thirty-two states have a Washington county. His birthday, February 22, is a legal holiday, which means that all federal, state, and city employees receive the day off from work. It is a day to remember how much one man could give to his country.

Washington's Birthday

Use these clues to fill in the crossword puzzle on the next page.

ACROSS

1. Washington was born in a _____.

4. George Washington became _____-in-chief of the American army.

6. As president, Washington wanted to create _____ for the United States.

7. Washington was the only person after the _____ period to have a state named after him.

10. George was _____ as a child.

12. George and his friends were taught by _____.

15. Washington's _____ was important to America winning the War for Independence.

16. George Washington was born in the state of _____.

17. _____ _____ were a favorite pastime on Washington's farm.

DOWN

2. Washington's birthday is a legal _____.

3. _____, state, and city employees have the day off from work on Washington's Birthday.

4. Washington took part in the convention that wrote the _____.

5. Washington grew wheat and _____ on his farm.

8. George Washington married Martha _____.

9. Washington was President of the United States for _____ terms.

11. George Washington's plantation was called _____ (abbreviation) _____.

13. As a youth, George worked as a land _____.

14. Some Americans asked Washington to become _____, but he refused.

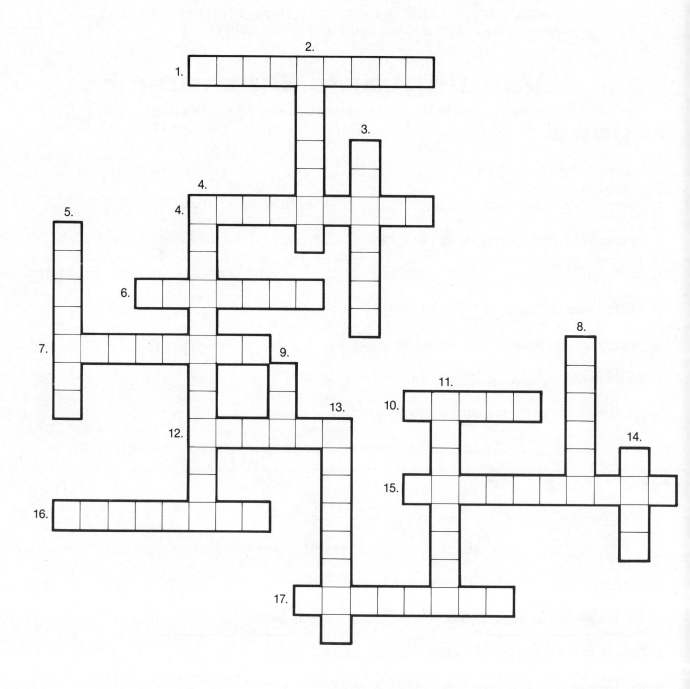

Washington's Birthday

Name_____

Each puzzle piece below contains an event that took place during George Washington's life. Cut out the pieces, and then arrange them from top to bottom in the order the events occurred.

When you're finished, you'll see that the pieces form a picture of our first president. You may want to paste the picture on another sheet of paper and color in Washington's features.

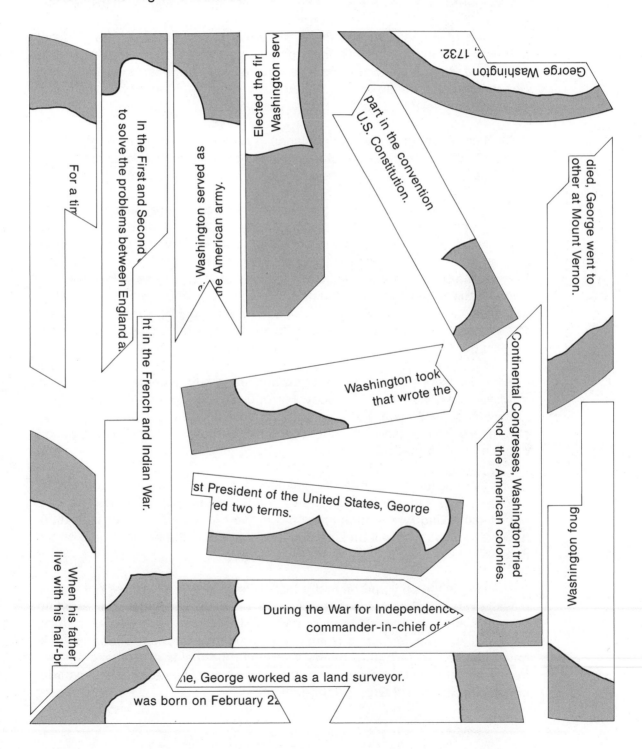

George Washington ... 2, 1732.

Elected the fir...
Washington serv...

part in the convention
U.S. Constitution.

died, George went to
other at Mount Vernon.

For a tir...

In the First and Second...
to solve the problems between England a...

... Washington served as
...he American army.

...ht in the French and Indian War.

Washington took
that wrote the

Continental Congresses, Washington tried
...nd the American colonies.

Washington foug...

...st President of the United States, George
...ed two terms.

When his father
live with his half-br...

During the War for Independenc...
commander-in-chief of ...

...ne, George worked as a land surveyor.

...was born on February 22...

Mardi Gras

Mardi Gras takes place each February or March on Shrove Tuesday, the day before Lent. Lent, the forty-day period of preparation for Easter, was for many years a time of strict fasting for Christians. On the day before the fast began, however, people held magnificent balls, parties, and parades. It was a time for loud and lively celebrations before the serious and solemn Lenten period. Today's Mardi Gras celebrations, like those long ago, are filled with excitement.

In parts of France, an enormous ox and a child known as the "king of butchers" star in the Mardi Gras parade. In southern France — as well as in Spain and Portugal — paraders toss flowers from brightly decorated carts. Spectators catch the flowers and then throw them back. At night, the French celebrate the holiday by going to masked balls.

On Saint Thomas in the Virgin Islands, a prince and princess reign over a special children's parade. All of the parade floats bear fairy tale themes, and everyone — babies, too — dons a fancy hat to join in the carnival.

On Shrove Tuesday, many Europeans bake splendid breads and cakes. In Denmark and Norway, children try to take bites of Shrovetide buns which are hung from the ceiling and swung back and forth. In England, people call the holiday "Pancake Day." Because they could not eat fat during Lent, people used to fry pancakes in order to use up any leftover fat in the house. A few towns in England still stage pancake contests on the holiday. In one, women contestants run while carrying a pan of pancakes. Each runner must flip the pancakes over three times during the race. The term "flapjack" may have come from this old English game.

French settlers in New Orleans, Louisiana held the first American celebration of Mardi Gras back in 1704. Today, Mardi Gras is a legal holiday in parts of Louisiana as well as in Alabama and Florida. The New Orleans Mardi Gras parade, which takes place at night, is certainly the most spectacular celebration of the holiday in the United States.

The parade follows about fifty smaller parades held during the previous weeks by organizations called "Krews." One of these organizations, the Rex, chooses the king for the nighttime parade. No one outside this organization, however, knows who will be king until he rides down the parade route on his float.

The king is the only person in the Mardi Gras parade who does not wear a mask. Even spectators wear masks and dress in costumes representing monsters, clowns, animals, and celebrities. There are many beautiful floats, some pulled by mules, some illuminated by gigantic torches. Often the floats have animated papier maché animals, serpents, mermaids, and other creatures from myth and history. Gala balls and parties take place after the parade, concluding the Mardi Gras celebration.

Mardi Gras

The following statements about Mardi Gras are either true or false. Circle the letter in the "True" column if the statement is true. Circle the letter in the "False" column if the statement is false. The first one is done for you.

Then put the circled letters on the numbered blanks at the bottom of the next page. Be sure to match the number of the sentence from which you take each letter with the number under the blank.

When you're finished, you'll discover the hidden Mardi Gras message.

	True	False
1. Lent is the name for the forty days before Easter.	(A)	E
2. Lent is a time to feast and make merry.	T	M
3. Shrove Tuesday is the last day of Lent.	S	R
4. A special children's parade takes place in the Virgin Islands.	T	N
5. In Denmark, children try to eat buns hanging down from the ceiling.	G	H
6. In Spain, a child takes the part of the "king of butchers."	U	I
7. Mardi Gras is not a legal holiday in any part of the United States.	E	S
8. French settlers first celebrated Mardi Gras in New Orleans in 1704.	E	A
9. Shrove Tuesday was called "Pancake Day" in England.	O	R
10. Long ago, Mardi Gras was a very quiet time.	F	H
11. In Spain and Portugal, carts are gaily decorated with flowers.	K	W
12. There is only one parade in New Orleans at Mardi Gras time.	C	D
13. The name of the king of the New Orleans Mardi Gras parade is always printed in the newspaper ahead of time.	J	U

Name_____

	True	False
14. Only the king of the New Orleans Mardi Gras parade wears a mask.	L	F
15. Some floats in the New Orleans parade have movable animals.	N	U
16. The New Orleans City Council selects the Mardi Gras king.	B	Y

Secret Holiday Message:

_ A _ _ _   _ _ A _   _ _ _ _ _ _
2 1 3 12 6   5 3 1 7   6 7 10 8 3 8

_ _ _ _ _ _ _ .   _ _ _ _ _ _ _ ,
4 9 15 6 5 10 4   5 8 4 16 9 13 3

_ A _ _ — _ _ _   _ _ _ _ _
2 1 7 11 16 9 13   3 8 9 13 4

_ _   _ _ _ _ _ !
9 14   7 6 5 10 4

128

Japanese Girls' Day

Japanese girls are happy on March 3 because it's a special holiday known as *Hina Matsuri,* Girls' Doll Festival. It is a day for parents to express their love for and pride in their daughters.

Once a year, girls unpack boxes of fifteen or more dolls wearing ancient costumes to represent the Japanese imperial court. These valuable festival dolls are available in stores, but often they are heirlooms handed down through the generations from mother to daughter.

The girls place the dolls on different shelves. On the top shelf stand the *Dairi-Sama* (emperor and empress dolls), dressed in ancient court costumes of silk. The emperor stands on the top shelf because of his great power. On the lower shelves are court ministers, ladies in waiting, musicians, and imperial guards. The dolls are surrounded by miniature replicas of imperial household furniture and dishes. All the dolls wear *sokutai,* a court-style dress. Girls whose families can't afford a set of dolls usually display just a single doll.

Since the girls put soft pink and white peach blossoms all around their dolls, the Doll Festival is often called the Peach Blossom Festival. The flowers symbolize the gentleness, sweetness, and peacefulness of girls. Recently, some dolls representing movie and baseball stars have joined the traditional dolls on the shelves.

No one knows exactly how the Doll Festival began. Some people believe that long ago dolls were part of a ceremony to worship the emperor. Others believe the dolls once represented human beings and acted as charms to protect people from sickness, disaster, and evil spirits. Families used to gather together in springtime to make crude straw or paper dolls. They rubbed the dolls against their bodies to transfer evil to the straw or paper figures. Then they threw the dolls into a stream or river, which carried the evil away.

During *Hina Matsuri,* girls wear bright colorful kimonos and invite friends over to a party. All the girls are very polite and observe the proper etiquette as they enjoy sweet rice cake (called *hishi mochi*) in layers of green, pink, and white. Instead of tea, the children sip *amazake* — a sweet, thick rice wine. After the party, the girls share their dolls.

Some Japanese-American families, especially those families whose grandparents came from Japan to the United States, also celebrate Girls' Day. Banks and ethnic stores in Japanese communities often display sets of dolls during the holiday. At the children's parties in America, the girls enjoy milk or punch with their cookies and cake instead of the traditional rice wine.

Japanese Girls' Day

Use these clues to fill in the crossword puzzle on the next page.

ACROSS

2. Peach blossoms symbolize _____, sweetness, and peacefulness.

3. On Girls' Day, Japanese parents express their love for and _____ in their daughters.

5. Japanese families celebrate Girls' Day in the month of _____.

8. _____ _____ means "Doll Festival" in Japanese.

10. Not all families can _____ a set of dolls to display.

11. A long time ago, people thought of dolls as _____ that would protect them from evil.

13. Early dolls were made out of paper and _____.

DOWN

1. Sweet rice cakes are called _____ _____.

4. On the top shelf stands the doll representing the _____.

6. Sometimes, festival dolls became _____, handed down from one generation to the next.

7. Instead of _____, children sip rice wine.

8. A long time ago, dolls were symbols of _____ _____.

9. All dolls wear _____, clothing of the imperial court.

12. The sweet rice wine is called _____.

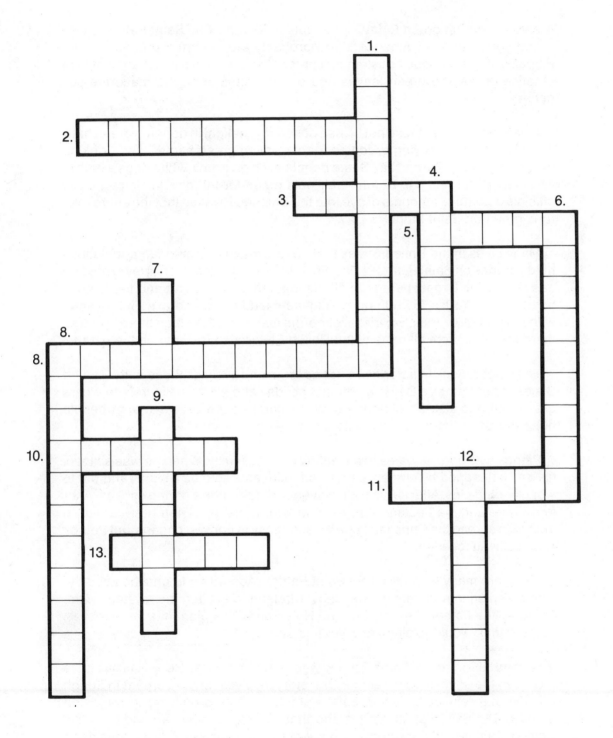

Saint Patrick's Day

Are your wearing green today? If the date is March 17 — Saint Patrick's Day —and you're an Irish-American, you probably are. Wearing green on Saint Patrick's Day is a popular custom that probably has its roots in the ancient Irish practice of burning green leaves and boughs each spring to make the soil richer.

Americans — even those not of Irish descent — delight in donning green hats, ties, or socks and waving green pennants, eating green bagles, and drinking green beer every March 17th. Some people even give their white dogs a bath in an emerald-colored dye to turn their pets green for the day. In Chicago, city officials pour huge amounts of dye into the Chicago River so that the entire river runs green on Saint Patrick's Day.

Many cities in the United States that have large Irish-American populations hold parades on Saint Patrick's Day. For over two hundred years, New York City has staged the largest parade of all. A mounted police escort and the famous band of New York's 165th Infantry Regiment lead the way down Fifth Avenue with Pat and Mike, their two Irish wolfhound mascots. More than three hundred marching units from all parts of the United States also take part in the parade.

The celebrations in Ireland are not as large and lively as those in the United States. Saint Patrick's Day is a national holiday and everyone in Ireland wears green, but it is also a religious holiday. Churches are crowded with people honoring Saint Patrick for his religious work in Ireland.

Patrick was born in Wales to a wealthy farming family. When he was sixteen, he was kidnapped by pirates, carried off to Ireland, sold as a slave, and put to work tending pigs. After six years in slavery, Patrick made a daring escape. After leaving Ireland, he became a priest and later a bishop. Then he returned to Ireland to spread the Christian faith. It wasn't easy to convert pagans, but Patrick eventually succeeded.

There are many legends about Saint Patrick. According to one, he used the little green shamrock that grows all over Ireland to explain the mystery of the Trinity — the Father, the Son, and the Holy Spirit. This plant has three leaves, Saint Patrick would explain, and yet it is one.

Legend also credits Saint Patrick with many miracles. He is said to have driven all the snakes from Ireland. One story involves an old serpent in Lough Dilveen that refused to leave. Saint Patrick left him, promising to return on Monday. But Saint Patrick forgot, and that serpent — now very old — is still waiting. Each Monday he comes up out of his lake and calls, "It's been a long Monday, Patrick!"

Saint Patrick's Day

The statements below about Saint Patrick's Day are either true or false. Circle the numbers of all the true statements. Then color the parts of the picture green wherever you find the numbers you circled.

When you're finished, you'll see a picture of something Irish.

1. Patrick was born in Wales.

2. When Patrick was sixteen, he ran away from home.

3. Patrick was sold as a slave to pirates in Wales.

4. As a slave, Patrick was put to work tending pigs.

5. After eight years of slavery, Patrick escaped.

6. Patrick went to Ireland to become a priest.

7. Later, Patrick returned to Ireland as a bishop.

8. Patrick succeeded in converting the Irish to the Christian faith.

9. According to legend, Saint Patrick drove the snakes from Ireland.

10. The biggest Saint Patrick's Day celebrations take place in Ireland.

11. Wearing green on Saint Patrick's Day is based on a Welsh custom.

12. Americans have invented imaginative ways to use green on Saint Patrick's Day.

13. Chicago holds the largest Saint Patrick's Day parade in the United States.

14. New York held its first Saint Patrick's Day parade in 1965.

15. In Ireland, Saint Patrick's Day is a national holiday.

Holi

One of India's happiest holidays comes each March. It is called *Holi,* the Festival of Spring.

The celebration begins on the eve of the holiday when people light huge bonfires which they believe are sacred. They pound drums and blow horns as they dance and shout, many whooping and beating their mouths with their hands. Some believe that the loud noises will drive away evil spirits. At dawn, when the fires die out, nothing of the old year is left but ashes. Each person marks his or her forehead with the ashes for good luck.

It is time to celebrate a new season. Everyone dresses in green, the color of spring. Young men put on yellow turbans and scarves, while children wear necklaces of white and yellow sugar. Family members press a bit of red powder on one another's foreheads as they exchange flowers and sweets.

Then the young people rush outdoors to continue the fun. They load water pistols and bamboo blowpipes with colored liquids or powders, and they shower their friends with bright colors. Some place pails of colored water around the streets for quick refills. In some cases, the young people form teams for the water games; win or lose, everyone gets drenched in a rainbow of crimson and saffron. All this fun is to greet the colorful promise of spring.

In the past, *Holi* play was even more adventurous. People were sent forth on foolish errands, similar to those of April Fool's Day. Men and women, young and old, were tossed into tubs of crimson water. No one could object to the dunking back then, but now it's illegal to dunk or throw color on anyone who might object!

Holi is an old festival which the Mongol Emperor Akbar made into a holiday that was supposed to unite the Indian people. Indians have always been separated by their caste system, which requires that people have contact only with those of their own social group. The Emperor felt that everyone would appear more equal when covered with a shower of splendid color.

Holi celebrations, which last from three to ten days, differ from one part of India to another. In the town of Besant, for example, people set up a twenty-five foot *chir* (pole) to begin the color play, and then they burn the pole at the end of the festival. In Orissa, colorful booths loaded with tempting wares crowd the market oval. People carry statues of gods from the temples in sedan chairs. There is lively music and dancing, and lamplights flicker as the sun goes down. In large cities like Bombay, groups of young people go out dancing with drummers leading the way.

Many delightful legends surround the festival of *Holi.* The bonfires recall the death of the terrible ogress Holika, the sister of a wicked king. This king hated his good son, Prince Pralhad, and twice tried to kill him. The ogress Holika decided to kill the prince with fire. Believing that fire could do her no harm, she took the boy into the flames herself. She sat down and held him on her lap. But the youngster was a follower of Lord Krishna, who saw what was happening and stepped in to save Prince Pralhad. Holika was left in the fire and burned to death.

Another legend tells of Holika's annual visit to the villages in the spring. The villagers dreaded Holika's coming because she always carried away some of their children. One spring, they decided to capture her. They shouted and beat noisy drums to confuse Holika. Then they seized her, heaped wood at her feet, and set the wood aflame. Holika never returned again.

One charming tale explains how the water-spraying began. The monkey god Hanuman was very small, but one day he managed to swallow the sun. The people were so sad about living in a dark world that the other gods suggested that they rub color all over each other and laugh. At first, people could not laugh because they were so sad. Finally, though, they mixed the color in water and ran around squirting each other. That did it; they began to laugh at last. Hanuman, who was watching all the squirting, thought it was so funny that he gave out one great laugh. As he laughed, the sun flew out of his mouth, and the world became bright once again.

Holi

Circle the letter next to the word or phrase that best completes each sentence below about *Holi*. Then put the circled letters on the numbered blanks at the bottom of the next page. Be sure to match the number of the sentence from which you take each letter with the number under the blank. The first sentence is done for you.

When you're finished, you'll find that the letters on the blanks spell a humorous answer to a *Holi* riddle.

1. *Holi* celebrates the coming of
   P. fire   (U.) spring   L. rain

2. Indians build bonfires on
   R. *Holi* eve   E. March evenings   J. the morning of *Holi*

3. Some Indians believe that making noise will frighten
   A. their friends   S. the emperor   P. evil spirits

4. On the day of *Holi*, young men dress in
   T. crimson   N. yellow and white   A. green and yellow

5. Young people decorate their friends with
   L. colored water   K. masks   W. sweets

6. People sometimes play water games
   I. indoors   R. around the bonfire   Y. in teams

7. Long ago, even older people used to be
   O. carried through the streets   N. tossed in tubs of water   H. tied to a *chir* (pole)

8. In India, *Holi* is
   O. celebrated in a variety of ways   C. a boring holiday
   T. celebrated in the same way all over the country

Name_____

9. A *chir* (pole) is
   G. built in Orissa   W. set up in Besant   M. burned on *Holi* eve

10. In Bombay, the celebration of *Holi*
    T. includes dancing and drummers   O. is very quiet   F. lasts only one day

11. Emperor Akbar wanted *Holi* to
    S. give the people a day of rest   E. break the caste system
    R. help frighten away evil spirits

12. According to legend, Holika was
    B. a wicked ogress   D. a monkey god   W. a friend of Krishna

13. Holika visited the villages to
    H. steal children   T. put out winter fires   X. bring rain

14. According to another legend, the world went dark because
    O. nobody could laugh   L. Hanuman was very small
    I. Hanuman swallowed the sun

15. People of India think of *Holi* as a day of
    H. thanksgiving   T. rest   D. fun

What would be a good business to open after *Holi*?

___ ___ ___ ___ ___ ___ ___ U̲ ___ ___ ___ ___ ___ ___ ___
8 3 11 7   4   5   4   1   7 15 2   6   4   7 15

___ ___ U̲ ___ ___ U̲ ___ ___ ___ ___ ___ ___ ___
6 8   1   9 8   1   5 15   7 8 10   12 11

___ ___ ___ ___ ___ ___ ___ ___
14 7   10 13 11   2 11 15

138

April Fool's Day

Have you ever heard of All Fool's Day? That's just another name for April Fool's Day, the first day of the month when people traditionally play jokes or send each other on impossible errands.

No one is certain how the custom of fooling people began. It may have started with an ancient Roman festival honoring the goddess Ceres. According to legend, Ceres heard the echo of screams from her daughter Proserpina who was kidnapped by Pluto and carried to the depths of the Earth. Ceres went off searching for her daughter, but it was a fool's errand because no one can find an echo.

The holiday may have started as part of the celebration of the spring equinox. Long ago, people thought that nature played tricks by suddenly changing from sunshine to rain showers. Or, April Fool's Day may have roots in the springtime Hindu fire festival of *Holi.* On the last day of *Holi,* unsuspecting people used to be sent on foolish errands.

Many people think that April Fool's Day as we know it today began in France during the reign of Charles IX. In 1564, Charles IX revised the calendar, changing the New Year's holiday. Until then, French people celebrated New Year's from March 25 to April 1, exchanging gifts on the last day of the celebration. Because news traveled slowly back then, many people didn't know for a long time that Charles IX had moved the holiday back to January 1. The ones who knew played tricks on people who continued with the March festivities. And people who agreed with the change in the calendar often sent trick gifts on April 1 to French men and women who did not like celebrating New Year's on January 1.

The French called their April Fool's pranks *poisson d' avril* (April fish), though no one knows exactly why. The phrase may refer to the way a fish gets tricked into biting a baited hook. Or it may be a reference to the zodiac; the sun leaves the house of Pisces on April 1. Today in France, bakeries decorate their windows with chocolate fish, and people mail postcards covered with drawings of fish to each other as jokes.

French, English, and Scottish settlers brought April Fool's Day to America. It has always been a favorite holiday of schoolchildren, who like to do things such as taping "Kick Me" signs to their friends' backs. Another prank involves tying a string to a wallet and then waiting for someone to pick it up. When the person bends over, the prankster pulls the string so that the wallet seems to run away from the unsuspecting person.

April Fool's Day begins National Laugh Week, which is a time for comedians to tell plenty of jokes. But to some people, April 1 isn't a time for laughter. These people refuse to marry or start a business on April 1, fearing bad luck. One good thing about April Fool's Day, though, is that it has remained over the centuries far less commercialized than many other holidays.

Name_____

April Fool's Day

Imagine that you have been swallowed by a *poisson d' avril* — an April's Fool's Fish. The numbers of the true statements below can guide you from "Start" out the mouth of the fish. Color the circles that contain the numbers of true statements to show your route back out the mouth of the April Fool's Fish.

1. Everyone in France liked the change in New Year's dates.

2. People are sent on foolish errands on the first day of *Holi*.

3. The April Fool's Day holiday began just a few years ago.

4. European settlers brought April Fool's Day to America.

5. April Fool's Day may have roots in the Hindu holiday of *Holi*.

6. Charles IX used to put "Kick Me" signs on his friends.

7. Schoolchildren love to play jokes on each other on April 1.

8. Ceres went on a fool's errand looking for her daughter.

9. April Fool's jokes in France are called *poisson d' avril*.

10. Some people refuse to marry on April 1.

11. French people mail postcards with drawings of pigs.

12. French bakeries decorate windows with chocolate fish.

13. National Laugh Week starts with April Fool's Day.

14. April Fool's Day may be tied to a celebration of summer equinox.

15. April Fool's Day is more commercial than most holidays.

16. No one is sure how the custom of fooling people began.

17. Proserpina was the daughter of Ceres.

18. Long ago, New Year's celebrations began on March 25.

19. Another name for April Fool's Day is All Fool's Day.

140

Name_____

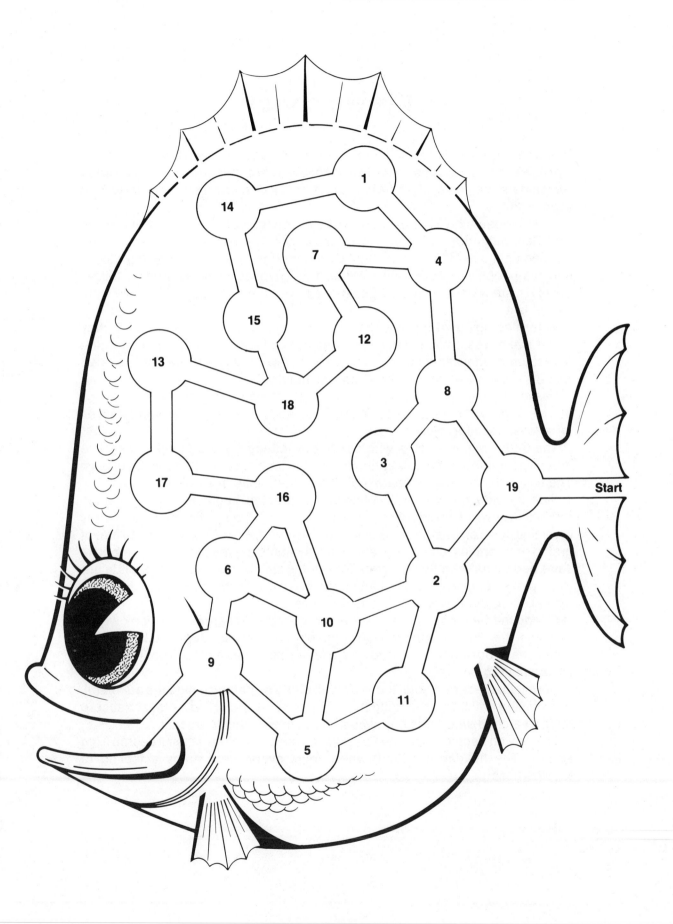

Start

141

Passover

Passover, one of the most important Jewish holidays, takes place in March or April. Passover comes from the Hebrew word *"Pesach."* The holiday remembers the Jews' flight from slavery in Egypt more than three thousand years ago.

Led by Moses, the Jews escaped in the hot desert sun. In front of them lay the Red Sea; behind them came the Pharaoh and his soldiers. The Jews were trapped until a miracle saved them. God parted the Red Sea, allowing Moses and his people to cross safely. When the Egyptian soldiers tried to follow, however, the waters of the Red Sea closed over them. The Jewish people were free at last.

When fleeing Egypt, the Jews had no yeast with which to bake bread. All they could make was a flat, unleavened bread called "matzoh." To remember the hardships of their ancestors in the desert, Jews today eat only unleavened bread — matzoh — during the Passover holiday.

Passover lasts seven or eight days. On the first night, families attend a service at a synagogue. On that night and the next, they gather together with relatives for a feast called a "Seder."

The Seder dinner begins with parsley or lettuce dipped in salt water. The green vegetable symbolizes springtime — the time of year when Passover falls. The salt water recalls the tears that Jews shed while in slavery.

Side by side on the Seder plate are a roasted lamb bone and an egg, reminding Jews of the sacrifices they made to God. A dish of bitter herbs serves to remind Jews of the bitterness of slavery. Also on the Seder table is a mixture of grated nuts, apples, cinnamon, and wine, symbolizing the mortar for the bricks Jews had to make while they were Pharaoh's slaves. Near the Seder plate are three pieces of matzoh, representing the cracker-like bread that the Jews ate while fleeing the Egyptians across the desert.

During the Seder dinner, family members read the *Haggadah,* a book which explains the Passover holiday. Young children at the Seder ask the four questions about the holiday, and then a family member reads the answers from the *Haggadah.*

During the Seder, an adult hides a small piece of matzoh called the *afikomen.* Then all the children go looking for it. This may be the world's oldest treasure hunt! The child who finds the *afikomen* receives a small present.

The Jewish people celebrate Passover as the beginning of their freedom from slavery. The holiday is a time when Jews everywhere enjoy a feeling of togetherness.

Yet, Passover has been an important holiday for other people, too. Everyone who treasures freedom can find a special meaning in Passover. American colonists compared King George of England to the Pharaoh, and they called George Washington the "American Moses" during the War for Independence. When asked to design a seal for the United States, Benjamin Franklin and Thomas Jefferson suggested showing the Jews crossing the Red Sea as they escaped from the Egyptians. And all during the hundreds of years in which blacks were slaves in America, they were inspired by tales of the Jews' escape from bondage. The spiritual "Go Down Moses" is evidence that black slaves knew the Passover story and longed for their own escape from slavery.

Passover

Complete each sentence about Passover by unscrambling the letters of the missing word. But beware! Each set of scrambled letters contains one extra letter. In the first sentence, for example, the missing word is *"Pesach,"* and the extra letter is "f."

As you complete the sentences, put the extra letters — in order — on the blanks at the bottom of the next page. When you're finished, you'll find that the extra letters spell another name for the Passover holiday.

1. Passover comes from the Hebrew word ____Pesach (+f)____.
   heaPsfc

2. Passover lasts seven or _____ days.
   g e t h e i

3. Passover takes place in March or _____.
   l s p i r A

4. The bitter _____ at the Seder remind Jews of the bitterness of slavery.
   s h b r e t

5. Passover celebrates the escape of the Jews from _____ more than three thousand years ago.
   y s i e l r v a

6. The Jews escaped from _____.
   p v t E y g

7. On the first night of Passover, most families attend a service at a _____.
   o y e a s g n u a g

8. The Passover feast is called a _____.
   d l e r e S

9. The cracker-like bread that Jews eat during Passover is called _____.
   t o h a m o z

10. Passover is an important holiday to everyone who treasures _____.
    e e f f m o d r

11. At the Seder, salt water symbolizes the _____ that Jews shed while in slavery.
    f r a s t e

12. During Passover, Jews eat only _____ bread.
    e d l u r e n n e a v

13. The book, read during the Seder to explain the meaning of Passover, is called the _____.
    a a a g g h H e d

14. The _____ is a piece of matzoh that is hidden during the Seder.
    f i m e e n o k a

15. Young children at the Seder ask the four _____.
    s e t o q s i u n d

16. Passover is a time when Jews everywhere enjoy a feeling of _____.
    o o e e e t t s s g h r n

17. _____ led the Jews out of slavery.
    s o e m s M

Passover is also called the

f̲ __ __ __ __ __ __ __   __ __ __ __ __ __ __ __ __
1 2 3 4 5 6 7 8   9 10 11 12 13 14 15 16 17

Easter Celebrations

Christians believe that Jesus Christ — the Son of God — rose from the dead on Easter Sunday. Celebrated today on the Sunday after the first full moon of spring, Easter has roots in pre-Christian festivals that welcomed the renewal of life in nature following winter.

The early Anglo-Saxons held a festival to honor their goddess of spring, Eostre. The Teutonic peoples celebrated with a festival of the spring sun, called Eastre. The name "Easter" probably came from one of these pagan feasts. As Christianity spread, the joy of the resurrection of Christ and the celebration of spring were combined into one holiday.

Many Easter customs go back many centuries. The custom of showing off new spring clothing, for example, dates back to early Christian times when converts to the faith were baptized at Easter and given new white robes to wear for eight days. The traditional Easter parade began in the fourth century. Roman Emperor Constantine ordered his subjects to dress in their finest and parade in honor of Christ's resurrection.

Although Christians around the world fill churches or attend special sunrise services on Easter Sunday, people in different parts of the world observe different Easter customs. In Europe, caroling is a popular Easter tradition. In Lithuania, the carol-singing children are called *Khristukas* (the little singers of Christ). In the German Tyrol, housewives compete to have the prettiest eggs to pass out to visiting carolers.

The practice of caroling first began with traveling actors. Today in England, amateur actors called pace-eggers go around performing simple plays in return for colored eggs.

There are traditional Easter foods, too. In parts of Germany, pretzels appear in the shape of the cross on which Christ died. Russian Christians bake an Easter cake with the letters "XB" on it; the letters mean "Christ is risen." Greek and Spanish people serve a bread decorated with Easter eggs.

In Alaska, the Athapascan and Aleut natives bake a bread called *"kulich."* If two people are on bad terms with each other, one may well send an Easter *kulich* as a token of apology. If the other person accepts the apology, he or she sends another *kulich* in return.

Easter decorations can be simple or elaborate. Flowers have always been associated with Easter. One of the most popular flowers for the holiday is the white trumpet lily — called the Easter lily — which came to the United States from Bermuda around 1880. Also back in the nineteenth century, the people of Germany and Switzerland began making fancy egg trees which looked much like Christmas trees. Children would decorate the trees with colored eggs, sugar figures, tinsel, and rabbits and lambs made of cake.

Easter is a day for religious observances, one of the most important of which is the sunrise service. The first sunrise service in America took place in Bethlehem, Pennsylvania in 1741. Sometimes, Easter religious observances are combined with fun. In Mexico, for example, adults and children join in banging and beating a *piñata* made to resemble Judas, the betrayer of Christ. In Hungary, boys sprinkle girls with a perfumed water shower on Easter Monday. In return for their "gift," the boys receive a holiday meal.

Easter Celebrations

Cut out the puzzle pieces at the bottom of this page. Then put them together so that they form the shape of an egg. The words along the edges are clues. By matching customs to the names of countries and peoples, you'll be able to figure out how the pieces should be arranged.

When you have all the pieces correctly assembled, paste them on the form below to complete your Easter egg.

The Easter Rabbit & Easter Eggs

The Easter rabbit with its basket of colored eggs is a familiar holiday symbol. The furry little creature became linked with Easter when people started figuring the date of the holiday by the phases of the moon. The rabbit has been associated with the moon since the days of the ancient Egyptians.

According to legend, the tale of a rabbit that passes out colored eggs began with a poor woman who had no money at Easter to buy sweets for her children. So instead, she dyed some eggs, hid them in a nest, and told her children to search for the eggs. While they were looking, the children spotted a huge rabbit in the bushes. Then they told their friends that the rabbit had brought the eggs in the nest. The story grew more detailed as it spread from person to person.

The Easter rabbit is part of many European holiday traditions. In some countries, it appears to have red or green fur. In others, it has the power to speak on Easter Day. In Germany, Switzerland, and Belgium, children place small nests in their gardens, hoping that the rabbit will come on Easter eve to fill the nests with eggs.

German immigrants to the United States brought their beliefs in the Easter rabbit with them. They built fires on Easter eve and told their children that the Easter rabbit was burning wild flowers to make dyes for his eggs. In Fredericksburg, Texas, some people of German ancestry still build fires on Easter eve. Then they tell their children the story that has been passed down through the generations.

Although the rabbit is the most popular bearer of colored eggs on Easter, it's not the only animal given that honor. Swiss children believe that the cuckoo brings the eggs, while Czech children look for a lark to bring their Easter eggs. In some parts of Germany, children await an Easter stork or a rooster that lays red eggs. Other German children think that an Easter fox delivers their eggs!

The egg, like the rabbit, was a symbol long before the Christian era. The ancient Egyptians, Persians, and Romans used to dye eggs and then eat them at spring festivals celebrating new life. Today, the egg is an important part of Easter all over the world. Only among Spanish-speaking people is the egg of little importance at Easter.

The Macedonians were the first Christians known to have used Easter eggs as a symbol of life in Christ. By the Middle Ages, coloring eggs at Easter had become very popular, with each color having a special meaning. Red was for the blood of Christ; yellow was for purity; and green was for fruitfulness.

To make their dyes, people would use different vegetables and herbs. Red cabbage and carrots produced red, while spinach and artichoke leaves made green. Onion skins could be made to yield tones of yellow and brown. In some European countries, people still make homemade Easter egg dyes from these plants, just as their ancestors did.

In Eastern Europe, especially in the Balkan countries and in the Ukraine, villagers used wax to create beautiful egg designs. Some of the patterns have been passed down from one generation to the next.

Perhaps the most famous Easter eggs of all were made in Russia by the jeweler Fabergé. In 1881, Tsar Alexander II was murdered, and his widow — the tsarina — became very depressed. For months she showed no interest in anything. Finally, the new tsar ordered Fabergé to make an unusual Easter egg that would surprise and delight the grieving woman.

Fabergé fashioned many Easter eggs over the years for the Russian royal family. They were not real eggs, of course. The most beautiful was carved from crystal. Most had jewels on the outside, and each had a surprise inside — a bird that popped out or a tiny ship floating on a sea of precious stones. Today, the Fabergé eggs are treasures to be seen in museums throughout the world.

Name_____

The Easter Rabbit & Easter Eggs

Cut out the sixteen egg halves. Then match the top halves above the line with the bottom halves below the line to complete eight facts about the Easter rabbit and Easter eggs. Finally, tape the matching halves together and color the eight eggs.

The first Christians to use eggs at Easter

Eastern Europeans

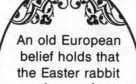

An old European belief holds that the Easter rabbit

The rabbit

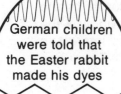

German children were told that the Easter rabbit made his dyes

Eggs are not an important part of Easter

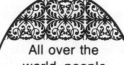

All over the world, people have made dyes

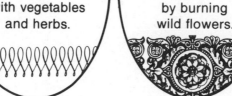

Swiss, German and Belgian children hoped the Easter rabbit

---

was an ancient symbol of the moon.

with vegetables and herbs.

by burning wild flowers.

were the Macedonians.

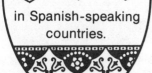

in Spanish-speaking countries.

use wax to create designs on eggs.

can speak on Easter Day.

would fill their nests with eggs.

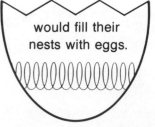

Easter Games & Contests

For hundreds of years, children in Europe and America have enjoyed Easter egg games and contests.

Egg Rolling. Egg-rolling contests may have begun for religious reasons. The rolling egg represented the rolling away of the stone that covered the tomb of Christ. Today, egg-rolling contests take place on grassy slopes, and they are purely for fun.

English children consider it good luck if their eggs roll down the hill unbroken. It's a sign of even better luck for a person if his egg breaks someone else's. In Holland, the person whose egg rolls the farthest receives a prize. The Germans give an award to the contestant whose egg rolls the fastest down a speedy track made of sticks.

In Egypt, children bowl red and yellow eggs toward another row of eggs. Whoever can crack one egg can claim them all. In the United States, children crowd onto the White House lawn on Easter Monday for the annual egg-rolling party.

Egg Gathering. In Germany and neighboring countries, children form egg-collecting teams. Each team has a "runner" and a "reader." While the reader gathers the eggs, the runner must cover a certain distance, sometimes from one village to the next. Runners can go on bicycles, on horseback, or on foot. In Belgium, the players are sometimes blindfolded, while in Holland, the runner must eat an apple that is floating in a tub of water while the reader collects the eggs.

Egg Tapping. In this game, each player holds an egg firmly in hand and uses it to tap another person's egg, trying to break it. In Holland, where the sport is called *eiertikken,* children line up with baskets of colored eggs. They use their eggs to break the eggs in another person's basket, but they must be sure that the only eggs they break are the same color as their own.

In Romania, visitors strike their red eggs against one held by the head of the household. As people tap eggs they exchange the greeting, "Christ is risen!" "He is risen, indeed!" The person whose egg remains unbroken the longest is supposed to have the longest life.

Egg Tossing. Egg tossing is a skill that requires practice. German children practice tossing eggs with a twist so that the eggs land in the grass spinning. Dutch children play a tossing game called "Egg Sales" in which one child sells an egg and the new owner throws it in the grass. If the egg does not break, it must be returned to the seller.

Egg Dances. In Holland, children dance inside a large circle of eggs. They try to work their way out of the circle without breaking any of the eggs. In England, egg dancing takes the form of egg hopping. In one version, blindfolded children hop among eggs, trying not to break any. In another version, the hoppers use their feet or sometimes a stick to break all the eggs they can.

Easter Games & Contests

The statements inside the Easter eggs below are either true or false. Color all the eggs that contain true statements. Then place the letters you find at the tops of the colored eggs on the blanks at the bottom of the next page. Make sure that you put the letters in order — starting with the top row and going row by row from left to right.

When you're finished, you'll complete the silly answer to an Easter rabbit riddle.

e
Egg gathering in Germany is usually done with a partner.
1

n
German children enjoy playing Egg Sales.
2

s
In Denmark, the runner must eat an apple.
3

g
Each year, there is an egg-rolling contest on the White House lawn.
4

g
Egyptian children roll eggs in a bowling game.
5

h
Sometimes, eggs are rolled on tracks of sticks.
6

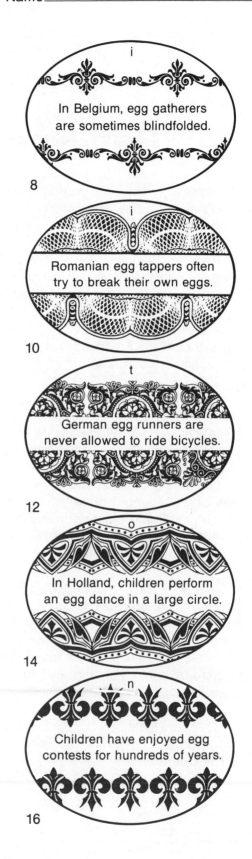

o — Swedish children enjoy the game of *eiertikken.*
7

i — In Belgium, egg gatherers are sometimes blindfolded.
8

m — English children enjoy egg hopping.
9

i — Romanian egg tappers often try to break their own eggs.
10

s — In England, children must never break an egg while hopping.
11

t — German egg runners are never allowed to ride bicycles.
12

a — German children toss eggs onto cement so they do not break.
13

o — In Holland, children perform an egg dance in a large circle.
14

r — In Holland, the one whose egg rolls fastest receives a prize.
15

n — Children have enjoyed egg contests for hundreds of years.
16

What must you do to get a lazy Easter rabbit to run faster?

You have to ___ ___ ___ ___ ___ ___ ___ ___ **!**

Pan American Day

On April 14, twenty-one countries in North, Central, and South America observe Pan American Day. The holiday — celebrated since 1931 — marks the birth of Pan Americanism on April 14, 1890.

Back in 1890, the International Conference of American States met in Washington, D.C. They laid the groundwork for an organization called the Pan American Union. Eventually, the Pan American Union became the Organization of American States (OAS). The OAS seeks to strengthen peace and security in the Western Hemisphere by creating better relations among the various countries of the Americas. It also provides a forum for settling disputes among the member countries.

Those member countries of the OAS include Argentina, Bolivia, Brazil, Chile, Colombia, Costa Rica, Cuba, the Dominican Republic, Ecuador, El Salvador, Guatemala, Haiti, Honduras, Mexico, Nicaragua, Panama, Paraguay, Peru, the United States, Uruguay, and Venezuela.

On April 14, these countries celebrate Pan American Day with folk songs and dances. Students from all over the Western Hemisphere travel to the Pan American Union Building in Washington, D.C. There, against a backdrop of twenty-one flags representing the member countries, the young people offer a program of entertainment.

Although Pan American Day is meant mainly to celebrate the bonds of friendship among the nations in the Western Hemisphere, it is also a day to pay tribute to one man: Simon Bolivar. Bolivar — called "The Liberator" — led the battle for independence in much of South America during the early part of the nineteenth century. Under his leadership, colonists in Venezuela, Colombia, Ecuador, Bolivia, Panama, and Peru fought to throw off the rule of Spain. After a long struggle, they were victorious.

There are statues of Bolivar in Washington, D.C. and in New York City. On April 14, important government officials lay wreaths before these statues to honor "The Liberator."

Pan American Day

Vacations are lots of fun

If you have the money and the time.

But if you cannot get away,

You can travel there in rhyme!

Look at a map of North, Central, and South America to help you complete each of the rhymes below.

1. A jet plane

   Can really "thrill ya."

   So can Brazil's capital —

   the city of ___ ___ ___ ___ ___ ___ ___ ___ .

2. Want to ski?

   Find a land that's hilly.

   Better go way

   Down south to ___ ___ ___ ___ ___ .

3. Need some things?

   Find a store.

   Surely there are some

   In ___ ___ ___ ___ ___ ___ ___ .

4. Its capital city

   Is Managua.

   Now guess the country.

   It's ___ ___ ___ ___ ___ ___ ___ ___ ___ .

5. Long time no see?

 What do you "say-o"?

 Uruguay's capital is

 The city of ___ ___ ___ ___ ___ ___ ___ ___ ___ ___ .

6. I like to travel.

 It's really "neat-o."

 What's Ecuador's capital?

 You bet, it's ___ ___ ___ ___ ___ .

7. In English, he's uncle.

 In Spanish, he's *tio*.

 In Brazil there's a city

 That people call ___ ___ ___ .

8. Airports can be hectic,

 With long, long waits.

 Isn't it nice to be home again

 In our own ___ ___ ___ ___ ___ ___ ___ ___ ___ ___ ___ ___ .

Songkran

The Water Festival, called *Songkran,* is Thailand's joyous welcome to spring. It is a three-day celebration (April 13-15) of the Buddhist new year.

Songkran parades feature enormous statues of Buddha that spray perfumed water onto the many happy spectators. Since the Water Festival comes at the hottest time of the year in Thailand, everyone enjoys the shower. The parades also include gilded floats and noisy bands. Girls in traditional Thai costumes, complete with cone-shaped headdresses, perform folk dances slowly and gracefully.

During *Songkran,* the sprinkling of water is a form of blessing. Children pour scented water into the hands of their parents as a sign of respect. At the *wat* (temple), families sprinkle perfumed water on the statue of Buddha. Family members dress in their best new clothes, but they remove their shoes before they enter the *wat.* During their visit, they offer rice to the monks. According to tradition, however, only males may hand an offering directly to a monk. Women and girls must lay their offerings on the floor in front of the monk or have a father or brother pass the gift of rice to the monk.

For young people, *Songkran* is also a time of play. They enjoy throwing water simply for the fun of it. They scoop up water from ponds and rivers to toss at their friends or to fill water pistols for more careful aim.

The Thai people perform acts of kindness during *Songkran.* They carry bowls of pet fish to a river and release the fish into the water. Some people even buy birds before the holiday so that they can set these creatures free, too.

Thais enjoy a special family meal on *Songkran.* Favorite dishes include beef or chicken curry, fried crisp noodles, chicken, prawns, and barbecued beef. Thai desserts (called *kanoms)* always contain coconut or rice, and they are served with a variety of tropical fruits.

Songkran marks a happy beginning to spring all over Thailand. Everyone wears flowers and dances to traditional Thai music. In the big cities as well as in the small towns and villages, a holiday queen reigns over the local celebration of the Water Festival.

Songkran

Circle the letter next to the words that best complete each statement below about *Songkran.* Then put the circled letters on the numbered blanks at the bottom of the next page. Be sure to match the number of the sentence from which you take each letter with the number under each blank.

When you're finished, you'll see that the letters spell the silly answer to a *Songkran* riddle.

1. *Songkran* is also known as the
   E. Festival of Spring   A. Water Festival   P. Festival of Buddha

2. *Songkran* lasts
   D. three days   F. one week   M. one day

3. *Songkran* takes place during Thailand's
   S. rainy season   T. hottest time of the year   N. vacation time

4. Thai folk dances are always
   P. performed outdoors   S. done in costume   H. performed slowly and gracefully

5. Families visit a *wat* to
   U. set the monks free   J. set fish free   O. honor the statue of Buddha

6. People set birds free on *Songkran* because
   E. they want to be kind   N. they consider the birds to be sacred
   S. it is the birds' mating season

7. Children show respect to their parents by
   N. pouring scented water into their hands   H. going with them to the *wat*
   B. removing their shoes

8. In Thailand, only males may
   H. enter a *wat*   V. sprinkle the statue of Buddha with water
   W. hand an offering to a monk

158

9. On *Songkran,* young people throw water on each other
   L. to show respect   I. because it is hot   P. for fun

10. All *Songkran* desserts
    G. are types of pudding   S. contain coconut or rice   O. are fattening

11. *Songkran* is celebrated
    I. in many parts of Thailand   K. only in Thailand's large cities
    R. only by Buddhist monks

Why did the thin man go to Thailand's Water Festival?

4	6	8	1	7	3	6	2	3	5	8	4	6	3

4	11	10	1	9	9	6	3	11	3	6

Songkran

Songkran is known as the Water Festival. In the word search puzzle below, you will find many words that relate to water. The words run horizontally (——), vertically (|), and diagonally (\ ). Circle each hidden word in the puzzle, and then fit it into the right grid of the three at the bottom of the page. The first one is done for you.

When you have all three grids filled with the hidden words, you'll have water, water, water!

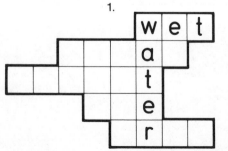

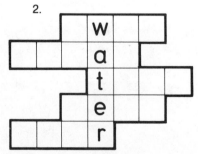

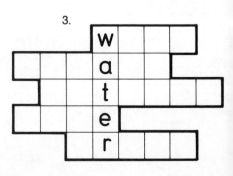

160

Arbor Day

Arbor Day is an April holiday dedicated to the preservation of useful, beautiful trees. This holiday encourages everyone to lend a hand in protecting the national forests. The word "arbor" means "trees" in Latin.

Trees have always been important to people, not only for their practical usefulness, but also as part of many traditions. In Mexico, long ago, the Aztecs planted trees for their newborn children as a sign of the strength they would achieve as they grew. In colonial times, a bride would transplant a tree from her father's garden to her new house in order to symbolize a great marriage to come. And, of course, we use the evergreen for Christmas trees and maypoles as people have done for centuries.

The Arbor Day holiday began with a man named J. Sterling Morton. Morton thought that the state of Nebraska didn't have enough trees. In 1872, Morton suggested that the state board of agriculture declare an annual tree-planting day and award prizes to the county that planted the most trees.

During the first Arbor Day celebration on April 10, 1872, Nebraskans planted more than one million trees! The event was such a success that the Nebraska legislature set April 22 (Morton's birthday) as Arbor Day. Today, Nebraska has the only national forest planted entirely by citizens of the state.

Soon other states, like Kansas and Tennessee, were celebrating Arbor Day, too. In fact, most states now observe Arbor Day, although they don't all celebrate it on the same day. Because of their differing climates, the states plant trees at different times of the year. Some states combine Arbor Day with other holidays. California, for example, celebrates Arbor Day and Bird Day at the same time. Mississippi celebrates Arbor Day as part of Conservation Week.

Canada, South Africa, Norway, France, Mexico, Spain, and Israel also celebrate Arbor Day, making it an international holiday. One of the most unusual Arbor Day celebrations of all time took place in the small town of Eynsford, England. The people of Eynsford planted shade trees in a pattern to spell out the lines of a poem by Alfred Lord Tennyson!

Arbor Day

Complete each of the following sentences about Arbor Day by filling in the missing word or words. Then put the letters in the numbered boxes on the blanks at the bottom of the next page. Be sure to match the number under the box with the number under the blank. The first sentence is done for you.

When you're finished, you'll see that the letters on the blanks spell the nickname of the state of Nebraska.

1. In ancient Mexico, Aztecs planted trees for newborn children as a sign of the

   | s | t | r | e | n | g | t | h |

   they would achieve.

   (1 under the "t")

2. Arbor Day began in the state of ☐ ☐ ☐ ☐ ☐ ☐ ☐ .

   (4)

3. Arbor Day is dedicated to the ☐ ☐ ☐ ☐ ☐ ☐ ☐ ☐ ☐ ☐ ☐

   (12)

   of useful, beautiful trees.

4. Nebraskans planted more than ☐ ☐ ☐   ☐ ☐ ☐ ☐ ☐ ☐ trees on

   (6)

   the first Arbor Day celebration.

5. The word "arbor" comes from the ☐ ☐ ☐ ☐ ☐ word meaning "trees."

   (9)

6. Not all ☐ ☐ ☐ ☐ ☐ ☐ celebrate Arbor Day on the same day.

   (10)

7. ☐ ☐☐☐☐☐☐☐ ☐☐☐☐☐ first
   ₂

suggested the idea for Arbor Day.

8. California celebrates Arbor Day and ☐☐☐☐ Day at the same time.
   ₁₁

9. We use the evergreen as a ☐☐☐☐☐☐☐☐ tree.
   ₇

10. Trees have played an ☐☐☐☐☐☐☐☐ role in traditions since
    ₅

early times.

11. In Eynsford, ☐☐☐☐☐☐ , people planted shade trees in a poetic pattern.
    ₈

12. Arbor Day celebrations show people how important it is to protect the national

☐☐☐☐☐☐☐ .
₃

Nebraska's nickname is the

T __ __ __ __ __ __ __ __ __ __ __
1 2 3 4   5 6 7 8 9 10 11 12

May Day

May 1 is May Day, a colorful holiday in many countries around the world. May Day celebrations have roots in ancient Roman practices. The Romans worshipped Flora, goddess of springtime, by carrying flowers to Flora's temple. Children wrapped garlands around the columns of the temple. As the Roman Empire conquered northern Europe, the Roman May Day practices spread to the conquered lands and mixed with traditions of other European peoples.

During the Middle Ages, May Day became a favorite holiday throughout northern Europe. Young people would gather in the woods, pick branches of "may" (pink and white hawthorn), and leave the branches at the homes of their friends. They also cut down one tall tree, and — after dragging the tree into the village — they decorated it with flowers, ribbons, and golden balls. Sometimes they painted the tree in colorful stripes. Then they crowned the prettiest girl in the village Queen of May and danced around the maypole.

In England, May Day became a time to honor the legendary outlaw, Robin Hood. Six men, dressed in green to represent Robin Hood's merry men, would launch a holiday parade by blowing horns. A man and woman dressed as Robin Hood and his queen, Maid Marian, would follow the merry men in the parade. Finally, there would be an archery contest, which was always won, of course, by Robin Hood.

Today in Europe, people still practice many interesting May Day customs. In France and Spain, May Day begins the month of the Virgin Mary, and children make small shrines in her honor. German and Swiss youths secretly plant May trees outside the windows of their sweethearts. In Greece, the schools close as people gather wild flowers to make spring wreaths.

In Italy, May Day is an important day for sports events and contests. In Scotland, some girls still get up at dawn on the first day of May to rub their faces with morning dew. The custom supposedly makes the young women beautiful for the men of their dreams. This Scottish May Day tradition was practiced for many years in parts of the Ozark Mountains in the United States.

Most American May Day festivals take place in parks and playgrounds. The center of attention is the maypole from which brilliantly colored streamers hang. Each child takes a streamer and walks in circles around the maypole, weaving in and out among the other children until the ribbons completely wrap the pole. Sometimes a May Queen reigns over the festivities.

Probably the most colorful May Day celebration in the United States takes place in Hawaii. There, May Day is known as "Lei Day," and people compete to create the most beautiful leis (garlands of flowers). A Lei Queen presides over the ceremonies as graceful hula dancers perform to the music of guitars.

May Day

Complete the sentences below by filling in the missing words on the blanks. Then place the letters above the numbered blanks on the matching numbered blanks at the bottom of the page. The first sentence is done for you.

   When you're finished, you'll find the silly answer to a riddle about the May Day maypole.

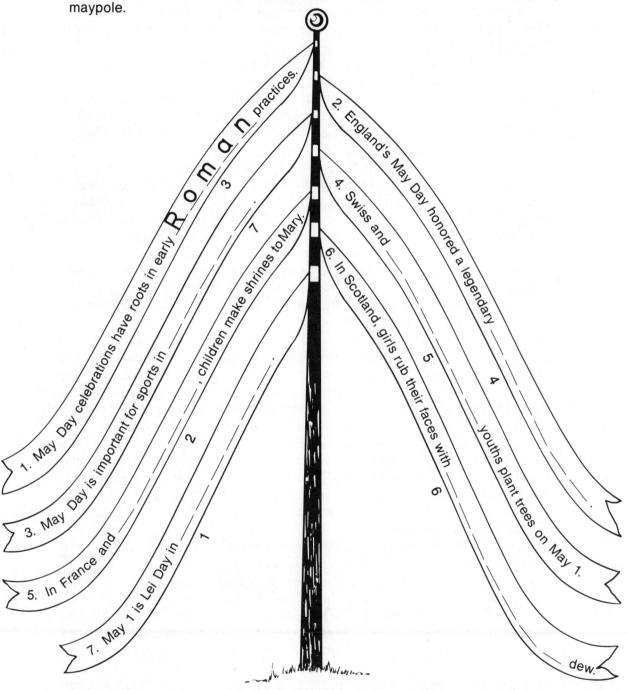

1. May Day celebrations have roots in early **R o m a n** practices.

2. England's May Day honored a legendary ___ ___ ___ ___ (4)

3. May Day is important for sports in ___ ___ ___ (3)

4. Swiss and ___ ___ ___ ___ ___ (5) youths plant trees on May 1.

5. In France and ___ ___ ___ (2), children make shrines to Mary.

6. In Scotland, girls rub their faces with ___ ___ ___ (6) dew.

7. May 1 is Lei Day in ___ ___ ___ (1) (7)

What did the baby maypole say to its mother when she got all wrapped up at the maypole dance?

$$\underset{1}{\rule{1cm}{0.4pt}}\ \underset{2}{\rule{1cm}{0.4pt}}\ \underset{3}{\text{m}}\ \underset{4}{\rule{1cm}{0.4pt}}\ \underset{5}{\rule{1cm}{0.4pt}}\ \underset{6}{\rule{1cm}{0.4pt}}\ \underset{7}{\rule{1cm}{0.4pt}}\ !$$

Cinco De Mayo

Cinco De Mayo is an important holiday in Mexico. It honors a battle the Mexicans fought in 1862 against the French.

The trouble started when Mexico owed money to many countries, and Napoleon III of France insisted that Mexico pay its debts immediately. To force the payment, the French leader sent an army of 6,000 soldiers to Mexico. Mexican General Zaragoza had only 2,000 soldiers when the two armies met at the city of Puebla.

For more than a week the French and Mexicans fought each other in driving rain and hail. Finally, on May 5, 1862, the battle came to an end. General Zaragoza and his troops were victorious! It was not the final victory against the French. As a matter of fact, French soldiers remained in Mexico for five more years. But the battle of Puebla showed the world that the Mexican people loved their country and were willing to fight for it.

Today in Mexico, *Cinco de Mayo* is a day filled with excitement. There are parades featuring military bands, and some towns even re-enact the famous battle with the French. The men dress as French or Mexican soldiers, and they charge to the rumble of cannon and rifle fire. It's all very noisy, but no one gets hurt. When a soldier runs out of blank ammunition, he "drops dead."

Some on the Mexican side wear skirts and flowered hats to play the women cooks and nurses who accompanied General Zaragoza's army. A few of these *soldaderas* carry guns to show that women also fought in the battle. The re-enactment ends with the generals from each side meeting in a sword fight. Of course, it is General Zaragoza who wins.

Then it is time for *fiesta*. Music fills the air as *mariachis* wander about playing their guitars, piccolos, and violins. Dancers, often in feathered headdresses and masks, perform traditional folk dances. The festivities continue into the night, when the sky glows with exploding fireworks. Some townspeople build a *castillo* (castle) of bamboo about a hundred feet high. Fireworks tied to each section go off in turn, forming pictures of flowers, birds, and fountains.

The part of the *fiesta* children enjoy most, however, is the *piñata*. The *piñata* is a clay pot filled with candy and covered with papier mache so that it has the shape of an animal. One by one, the children put on a blindfold and swing a stick at the *piñata* — which dangles in the air from a rope. When someone finally hits and breaks the *piñata,* all the children scramble to get their share of the goodies that tumble to the ground.

Although *Cinco de Mayo* is a Mexican holiday, it is also popular in the southwestern portion of the United States. Many people of Mexican ancestry live in that section of our country. Each year, for example, the twin border cities of Nogales, Arizona and Nogales, Mexico hold a joint celebration of the holiday, with parades, dances, music, and so forth. Mexican musicians and dancers also perform in parks in San Antonio, Texas on May 5. In Los Angeles, California, the city hosts Mexican dancers and orchestras and sponsors a flag ceremony.

At Canyon Elementary School in Los Angeles, the holiday has a special meaning. Back in 1880, Mexican landowners donated the land for the school on one condition: Every year a *Cinco de Mayo* celebration would be held there. The school has lived up to the agreement, trying to hold the most elaborate holiday celebration on May 5 of any school in the city.

Cinco De Mayo

Complete each sentence below by circling the letter next to the correct word or phrase. Then put the circled letters on the blanks at the bottom of the next page. Be sure to match the number under each blank with the number of the sentence from which you take each circled letter. The first sentence is done for you.

When you're finished, you'll have the answer to the riddle: What is the best shape for a *piñata*?

1. *Cinco de Mayo* is celebrated in
   B. France   D. Spain   A. Mexico

2. The holiday honors a battle fought against
   T. France   F. United States   L. Spain

3. The battle took place
   E. almost 200 years ago   U. less than 100 years ago   O. more than 100 years ago

4. The Mexican army was led by General
   C. Napoleon   N. Puebla   K. Zaragoza

5. The battle lasted for
   E. more than a week   A. a few hours   H. almost a month

6. On May 5, some Mexican towns re-enact the
   W. fiesta   V. fireworks display   U. battle

7. A fiesta may include music played by
   G. Indians   S. *mariachis*   M. children

8. The part of the fiesta children enjoy most is the
   P. fireworks   R. dancing   I. *piñata*

9. The section of the United States where *Cinco de Mayo* is a popular holiday is the
   B. Southwest   P. Northwest   S. Midwest

10. Nogales, Mexico joins in celebrating the holiday with a U.S. city in
    Z. California   Y. Texas   Q. Arizona

11. *Cinco de Mayo* is important to the Mexican people because on that day
    D. Mexicans showed their love for their country
    F. the French were driven out of Mexico
    G. Mexico was able to pay all its debts

12. The land for Canyon Elementary School in Los Angeles was a gift from
    R. Napoleon III   P. City Hall   C. Mexican landowners

What Is The Best Shape For A *Piñata*?

A __ __ __ __ , __ __ __ A __ __ __
1 11 6 12 4   9 5 12 1 6 7 5

__ __ __ __ __ __ __ __ __ __ __
8 2 8 7 10 6 8 12 4 2 3

__ __ A __ __
10 6 1 12 4

Tango-No-Seku

May 5 is *Tango-No-Seku* in Japan, a day when parents give thanks for their healthy sons. In a ceremony that is supposed to help their sons grow up strong and brave, parents erect a tall bamboo pole in the garden or on the roof. They attach a cloth — painted with a devil's face — to the top of the pole — to ward off any harm that might come to their boys.

Underneath the cloth is a huge kite made of black paper in the shape of a carp. A hoop in the carp's mouth catches the wind so that the fish looks as though it is swimming in air. The highest and largest carp kite stands for the oldest boy in the family. Below it are smaller red kites that represent the younger brothers in the family.

The carp kites are supposed to make boys act like the spirited fish, which have the power to swim up streams and even climb waterfalls. The carp — called *koi-nobori* in Japanese — is a symbol of courage, power, and determination. In some places in Japan, small boys crawl through the paper carp kites from mouth to tail for good luck.

Tango-No-Seku may have begun as a rural festival in ancient times. In early May, farmers used bright flags decorated with ugly figures to drive away insects. Later on, the ugly figures were replaced by pictures of samurai warriors. Eventually, Japanese parents began to hang flags indoors to teach boys about manliness and to keep them safe from evil. Carp flags replaced warrior flags as symbols around 1772.

According to another story about the festival's beginnings, a Japanese prince — while in a garden of blooming iris flowers — asked for divine help in fighting off invaders from Mongolia. When Japan won the war, people felt that the prince's prayers among the iris flowers had brought good luck and victory. They began to decorate the eaves and doorways of their houses with iris stems to protect against fire and evil. Boys bathed in steaming water in which there were long strips of sword-shaped, sweet-smelling iris leaves. The leaves supposedly helped the boys develop a brave warrior spirit. Many Japanese families still grow the iris flower, though it is no longer common to decorate the house with iris or to have boys take iris baths.

On festival day, boys eat *kashiwa mochi* — rice cakes filled with a sweet bean paste and wrapped in dried oak leaves. Between banners and streamers on shelves, the boys display a set of warrior dolls. In America, the newborn sons of Japanese-American parents receive a doll as the start of their collection.

After World War II, *Tango-No-Seku* was renamed *Kodomo-No-Hi* (Children's Day) to honor both boys and girls. Although the name was changed, the holiday continues to be observed in the traditional manner of a day for boys.

Tango-No-Seku

The following sentences are either true or false. Put a "T" on the blank if the sentence is true. Put an "F" on the blank if the sentence is false.

Then shade the picture parts with a pencil wherever you see the number of a true sentence. When you're finished, you'll see a hidden picture of a *Tango-No-Seku* symbol.

1. The Japanese word for carp is *koi-nobori*. .... _____

2. Parents are thankful for healthy sons on *Tango-No-Seku*. .... _____

3. On *Tango-No-Seku,* parents hope their sons will fly a kite well. .... _____

4. The youngest boy in the family receives a large black kite. .... _____

5. Carp are lazy fish. .... _____

6. For good luck, boys crawl through the carp-shaped paper kites. .... _____

7. Another name for Children's Day is *Kodomo-No-Hi*. .... _____

8. Boys eat puffed wheat cakes filled with sweet honey on the holiday. .... _____

9. The carp stands for courage and strength. .... _____

10. Japanese parents hope that their boys will develop determination and strength throughout life. .... _____

11. The festival began when a prince used a cloth picture of a samurai warrior's face. .... _____

12. Bathing in steaming water with iris leaves was supposed to make boys become as brave as warriors. .... _____

Name

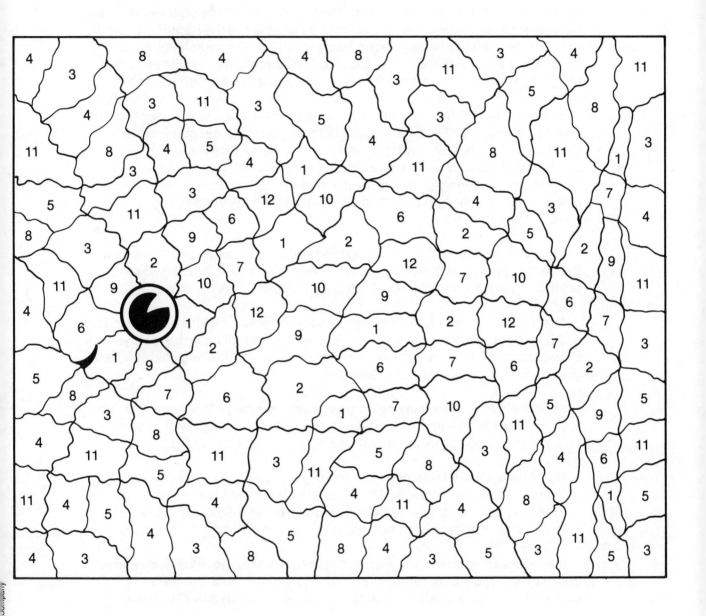

171

Urini Nal

Do you wish there were a holiday especially for children? The children in Korea have one. Known as *Urini Nal,* it is celebrated on May 5 in the Republic of South Korea. This national holiday began back in 1919 at the suggestion of Chung Hwan Bang, who felt that children deserved one day of their own in return for the obedience and respect they were expected to give all through the year.

Schools close for *Urini Nal* so that parents can plan special activities for their children to enjoy. In Seoul, the capital city of South Korea, admission to the Children's Park is free, and the rides are open to everyone. Professional dancers perform traditional circle dances as well as the popular Drum Dance. Sometimes the young girls join in the dances. Large audiences gather for exhibitions of wrestling (*sirem*) and the martial arts (*taekwondo*). Tug-of-war is another favorite sport.

Boys and girls also delight in the painting and creative writing contests held in the parks. The competitions require drawing with fine brush strokes and composing poems and stories. The contest winners receive prizes.

At special *Urini Nal* plays and puppet shows, Korean children enjoy stories about long ago. Back then, a royal family ruled the land. Often in these plays and shows, a prince gives a long speech on the importance of strong character and good habits. The children listen attentively.

Korean children enjoy playing on swings. In rural areas, they have a contest that involves a bell hung between two poles opposite a swing. Anyone who can swing high enough to kick the bell and make it ring wins a prize.

All through *Urini Nal* children find plenty of good things to eat. Cake shops give away rice cake favors, and vendors offer a variety of goodies — Korean barbecued meat, hot dogs, and even popcorn. A pickled cabbage treat with pine nuts and chestnuts is a special favorite.

After all these festivities, children and their parents can go to the theater to see free movies. Then they return home for more treats that the mothers have prepared to provide a happy ending to *Urini Nal,* the Korean Children's Day.

Urini Nal

Fill in on the fans below the various activities children enjoy on *Urini Nal.*

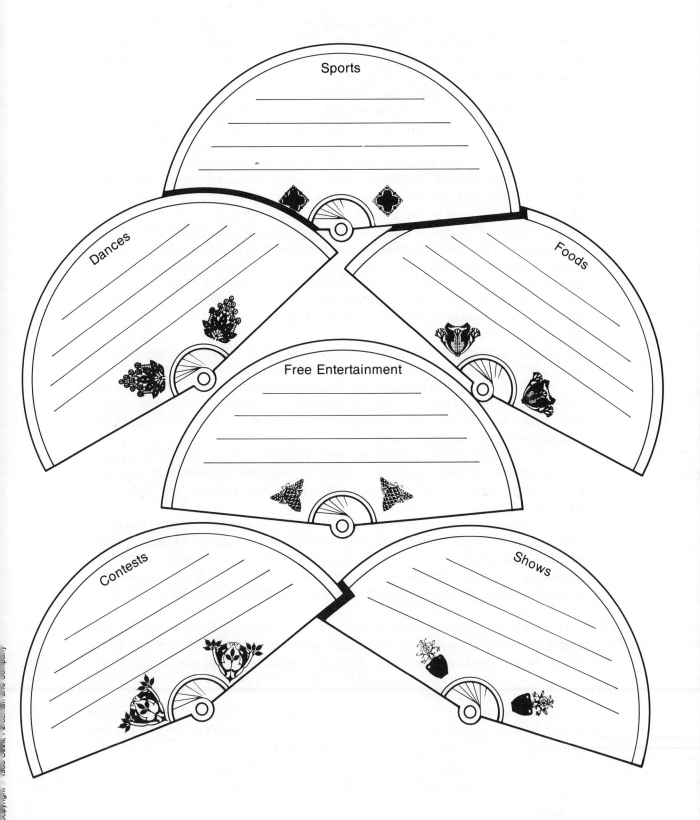

Pista Ng Anihan

Pista Ng Anihan — the Philippine celebration of a plentiful harvest — takes place on May 15, the feast of Saint Isidro. Isidro was a twelfth century Spanish farmer who became the patron saint of harvests. *"Pista"* comes from the Spanish word *"fiesta."*

To prepare for *Pista,* townspeople decorate their homes. Everyone tries to outdo his neighbor's decorations, hanging corn, coconuts, and fruit in windows and doorways. Families make interesting designs out of *kiping* (powdered rice), cutting it into thin strips, molding it into leaf shapes, and dyeing it in bright colors.

Sometimes, an owner decorates his home to show his occupation. A shoemaker, for example, might make an original display from the tools and materials of his craft. Many houses display *anoks* in different poses. *Anoks* are straw figures dressed in old clothes to represent farmers.

At noon on the day before *Pista,* the church bells ring to signal the beginning of the celebration. Then firecrackers start exploding and bands play. Teams from neighboring towns compete in basketball, softball, and volleyball. A parade marches down streets lined with bamboo arches that have candy, fruit, and bright paper streamers hanging down from them. When the parade is finished, the people of the Philippines attend church services to give thanks for the bountiful harvest.

That night, *Pista* Eve, the *Pista* Queen and her court reign over a dance in the town plaza. The most colorful dance, the Tinikling (Bamboo Dance), is named for the Tinikling bird — a creature which is always a threat to the rice harvest. People representing the birds dance between two bamboo poles that people clap to the beat of the music. The people clapping the poles represent the farmers trying to capture the birds.

Excitement fills the air on *Pista* morning. Many people go first to church and then to colorful field events. Eager young people at the field events compete in catching greased pigs, climbing greased poles, and playing *sips* (a type of badminton).

In some small towns, carabao (water buffalo) play a special role in the *Pista* celebration. Farmers wash, groom, and decorate their carabao with flowers and ribbons. Then they take the animals to the churchyard to be blessed. Without this beast of burden, the farmers would have no harvest. At *Pista,* the carabao take part in parades and races. Some even perform tricks they have practiced for months.

Friends and relatives gather at noon for the *Pista* feast. *Lechon* (barbecued pig) is the main dish, served with green papaya, *bibingka* (rice cakes), and other foods. In the evening there is a great procession. People carrying lighted candles sing and pray as they march through the streets. A statue of Saint Isidro is carried at the front of the procession.

The procession marks the end of *Pista Ng Anihan.* Once the procession is over, children race to the decorated bamboo poles and quickly strip away the goodies.

Pista Ng Anihan

Complete each sentence below by unscrambling the letters of the missing word and writing the word correctly on the blank at the right. But beware! Each set of scrambled letters contains one extra letter. Write the extra letter on the short blank at the far right. The first sentence is done for you.

Then put the extra letters on the numbered blanks at the bottom of the next page. Be sure to match the number of the sentence from which you take each extra letter with the number under the blank.

When you're finished, you'll see that you've written a short poem about *Pista Ng Anihan.*

1. *Pista Ng Anihan* is a holiday of the **n P p i h p s i i e l**........ ___Philippines___   I

2. The holiday takes place on the feast of Saint **d o s I r i y.**..... _____ ___

3. *"Pista"* comes from the **f S i h n a p s** word *"fiesta."*........... _____ ___

4. *Pista Ng Anihan* celebrates a good **a r r e h v t s.**.............. _____ ___

5. People decorate their **o e m h d s** for the holiday............... _____ ___

6. Straw figures called **k h a o s n** represent farmers............. _____ ___

7. Poles of **o o b m o a b** line the streets............................ _____ ___

8. The **u m c r h h c** bells announce the beginning of the celebration... _____ ___

9. There is a **a b p a d r e** on the afternoon before *Pista.*........ _____ ___

10. Teams compete in basketball, volleyball, and **f a l l n s o t b.**.. _____ ___

11. The *Pista* **e n e c u Q** reigns over the dance. .... _____ ___

12. A popular dance is the **k i g T l i n i e n.**.......................... _____ ___

13. The **c s d p r a n e** represent birds.................................... _____ ___

14. People clapping poles represent farmers trying to **t u c s r a e p** the birds... _____ ___

15. On the *g n a m i n o r* of *Pista,* people again go to church. .... _____ ____

16. In some towns, farmers honor their *b a c o a r a u..* .... _____ ____

17. Field events include catching *s r a g e g e d* pigs. .... _____ ____

18. The main dish at the feast is *e i l h n o c* (barbecued pig). .... _____ ____

19. *t k n i B g b i a* is a favorite food made of rice. .... _____ ____

20. At the end of the evening, children carry away *o o v i e d s g* hanging from the bamboo poles. .... _____ ____

$\overline{13}\ \overline{18}\ \overline{14}\ \overline{19}\ \overline{15}\ \ \overline{10}\ \overline{17}\ \ \overline{15}\ \overline{10}\ \overline{18}\ \overline{6}\ \overline{15}\ \overline{10}$,

$\overline{15}\ \ \overline{19}\ \overline{18}\ \overline{8}\ \overline{12}\ \ \overline{19}\ \overline{7}\ \ \overline{3}\ \overline{12}\ \overline{15}\ \overline{14}\ \overline{19}$

$\overline{15}\ \overline{10}\ \overline{5}\ \ \overline{13}\ \overline{1}\ \overline{15}\ \overline{2}$.

$\overline{9}\ \overline{12}\ \overline{11}\ \overline{15}\ \overline{16}\ \overline{14}\ \overline{12}\ \ \overline{19}\ \overline{6}\ \overline{12}$,

$\overline{6}\ \overline{15}\ \overline{4}\ \overline{20}\ \overline{12}\ \overline{14}\ \overline{19}\ \ \overline{14}$

$\overline{9}\ \overline{7}\ \overline{16}\ \overline{10}\ \overline{19}\ \overline{18}\ \overline{3}\ \overline{16}\ \overline{1}$,

$\overline{19}\ \overline{6}\ \overline{12}\ \overline{2}\ \ \overline{15}\ \overline{1}\ \overline{14}\ \overline{7}\ \ \overline{14}\ \overline{19}\ \overline{7}\ \overline{13}$

$\overline{19}\ \overline{7}\ \ \overline{13}\ \overline{4}\ \overline{15}\ \overline{2}$.

Mother's Day History

We've been celebrating Mother's Day in the United States on the second Sunday in May ever since 1914. The custom of honoring mothers, however, goes back thousands of years. Our modern holiday draws upon traditions from many parts of the world.

In ancient Phrygia (in Asia Minor), people honored the goddess Cybel as the mother of all gods and the symbol of motherhood. During the festival dedicated to Cybel, people would sing, dance, and march in beautiful parades. Later, the Romans honored a goddess they called *Magna Mater,* or Great Mother. The Romans believed the goddess helped them defeat enemies in battle.

Still later, the Christian church came to be known as the Mother Church. In a special celebration held once a year, people would bring gifts and flowers to honor the Mother Church.

During the Middle Ages, some children left home to become apprentices. On one Sunday each year, however, the children were allowed to visit their mothers. On Mothering Sunday, as it came to be called, children gave their mothers a small gift or a "mothering cake" (a rich and tasty fruit cake). They also helped their mothers with household chores.

The people who settled in the New World were too busy working to celebrate Mothering Sunday. It wasn't until a woman named Anna Jarvis came along that a special day for mothers came into existence in the United States.

Anna Jarvis loved her own mother dearly. After her mother died in 1905, Anna wrote to religious and government leaders, pleading to have a day set aside for honoring mothers. Her efforts led to the first Mother's Day celebration on May 12, 1907, in Grafton, West Virginia.

Since her mother had been fond of carnations, Anna Jarvis suggested that people wear either a white or a red carnation on Mother's Day. The white carnation was to honor a mother who had died, while the red carnation was to honor a mother still living.

On May 8, 1914, the U.S. Congress passed a resolution establishing the second Sunday in May as Mother's Day in every state. President Wilson signed the resolution into law the following day, and Mother's Day has been a national holiday ever since. In 1934, the Post Office printed a special Mother's Day stamp (picturing "Whistler's Mother" and a bowl of carnations) to honor mothers on their day.

Anna Jarvis died without ever becoming a mother herself, but she did give birth to a holiday that is celebrated every year in many countries around the world.

Mother's Day History

Complete each statement about Mother's Day by filling in the missing word. Then find and circle each missing word in the word search puzzle. Look carefully! The words may be spelled in any direction, even backwards.

After you find all the words in the word search puzzle, put the unused letters on the blanks at the bottom of the next page. Be sure to put the letters on the blanks in the order they appear in the puzzle, starting at the top and going row by row, left to right, down to the bottom row.

When you're finished, you'll find that the extra puzzle letters spell out a secret holiday poem.

1. In the United States, we celebrate Mother's Day on the _____ Sunday in May.

2. In ancient _____, the goddess _____ was honored as the mother of all gods.

3. The _____ also honored a mother goddess.

4. The Romans called their mother goddess *Magna* _____.

5. Christians brought gifts and _____ to honor the Mother Church.

6. In the Middle Ages, children visited their mothers on _____ Sunday.

7. Anna _____ started Mother's Day in the United States.

8. President _____ signed a resolution making Mother's Day a national holiday.

9. Grafton, _____ _____ was the site of the first Mother's Day celebration in America.

10. The founder of Mother's Day suggested that people wear a _____ or white

    _____ on the holiday.

11. In 1934, the U.S. Post Office issued a special _____ to honor all mothers.

a	m	a	t	e	r	h	f	a	p
c	p	p	m	a	t	s	l	y	m
a	y	m	o	r	t	h	o	e	o
i	r	b	s	e	d	a	w	y	t
n	t	o	e	d	m	o	e	t	h
i	h	e	r	l	s	e	r	v	e
g	s	j	a	r	v	i	s	e	r
r	e	r	y	w	h	e	a	r	i
i	c	a	r	n	a	t	i	o	n
v	o	e	o	s	i	t	g	b	g
t	n	a	m	c	k	h	y	a	v
s	d	e	a	f	u	n	r	n	o
e	w	o	n	r	k	n	h	o	c
w	i	l	s	o	n	a	p	r	e

A Secret Holiday Poem

__ __ __ __ __ __ ,

__ __ __ __ __ __ __ __ __ __

__ __ __ __ __ __ __

__ __ __ __ __ __ __ __ __ __ .

__ __ __ __ __ __ __ ,

__ __ __ __ __ __ __ ,

__ __ __ __ __ __ ,

__ __ __ __ __ __ __ .

179

Mother's Day Celebrations

Although it is not celebrated on the same day everywhere, Mother's Day is a holiday in many other countries. It was largely through the efforts of Anna Jarvis that Mother's Day became an international holiday.

The people of Denmark, Italy, Australia, Belgium, and Turkey celebrate Mother's Day on the second Sunday in May — just as people in the United States do. In Africa, however, Mother's Day falls on the first Sunday in May. In Argentina, it's the second Sunday in October, while Norwegians celebrate Mother's Day on the second Sunday in February.

In Yugoslavia, the holiday we know as Mother's Day is called *"Materice,"* and it comes two weeks before Christmas. In Lebanon, Mother's Day falls on the first day of spring.

The people of India celebrate two different kinds of Mother's Day holidays. The Christians in India celebrate a holiday much as the people in the United States do. The Hindus of India, however, observe a ten-day festival in October called *"Durga Puja."* *Durga* is the most important Hindu goddess in India. She has ten arms and carries a weapon in each arm to destroy evil.

During the first nine days of the festival, Hindu people bring presents to the temple of *Durga.* On the tenth day, they carry an image of the goddess to the river, and they place it on a boat. While some of the people row the boat out to the middle of the river, the others watch from the river bank. When the boat reaches the middle of the river, the people on board hurl the image into the water, and everyone shouts: "Victory to the Divine Mother. Victory to *Durga.*" Then they all return to their homes, where children wish their mothers happiness and good luck and present them with a small gift.

In France, Mother's Day takes place on the last Sunday in May. It is a family holiday in France, and the whole family — including grandparents — gathers together and eats a big meal. At the end of the meal, all the mothers in the family receive a beautiful cake that looks like a bouquet of colorful flowers.

Mother's Day in Sweden is also a family holiday, but it is different in one important way. The Red Cross in Sweden makes the holiday especially memorable for some mothers. The organization sells plastic flowers to raise enough money to send deserving mothers on a vacation!

In Portugal and Spain, Mother's Day falls on December 8. In both countries, the holiday is closely tied to the Church. The people of Portugal and Spain honor not only their own mothers on the holiday, but they also pay tribute to Mary, the mother of Jesus.

Mother's Day Celebrations

Use these clues to fill in the crossword puzzle on the next page.

ACROSS

2. In _____ they celebrate Mother's Day as we do in the United States.

3. The Hindus of India have a ten-day Mother's Day festival called

   _____ _____.

4. In France, family members gather on Mother's Day for a big _____.

5. Yugoslavians celebrate Mother's Day two weeks before _____.

9. In Sweden, Mother's Day is a _____ holiday.

10. There are _____ kinds of Mother's Day celebrations in India.

11. The _____ _____ in Sweden sells plastic flowers for Mother's Day.

DOWN

1. Hindu children wish their mother _____ and good luck on Mother's Day.

2. Through the work of _____ _____, Mother's Day is now celebrated in many countries.

3. Mother's Day is celebrated on _____ days in different countries.

5. Mother's Day in Portugal is closely tied to the _____.

6. Mother's Day in Yugoslavia is called _____.

7. Not all countries celebrate Mother's Day on the same _____.

8. In France, mothers receive a cake that looks like a bouquet of _____.

Name_____

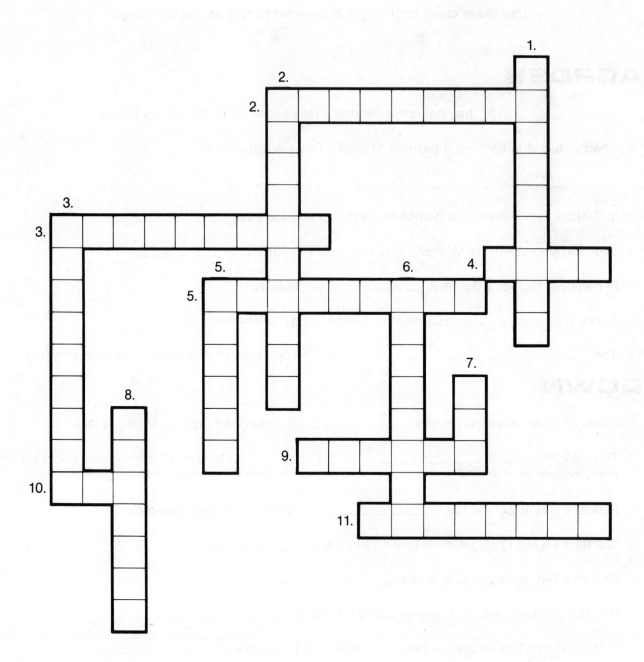

Memorial Day

Memorial Day, observed on May 30 or on the Monday closest to that date, began as a day to remember those who died while serving the United States. In recent years, this day of remembrance has been extended to include all relatives and friends who are no longer living. The custom of honoring the dead has its roots in many cultures, including those of the ancient Greeks and Romans.

In the United States, Memorial Day goes back to the time of the Civil War. In 1866, a druggist named Henry C. Welles suggested decorating the graves of the soldiers who had died during the Civil War. Since Welles lived in Waterloo, New York, the U.S. House of Representatives in 1966 honored Waterloo as the "Birthplace of Memorial Day."

In the same year Welles made his suggestion, the women of Columbus, Mississippi honored the Civil War dead in their cemetery by placing flowers on the graves of both Confederate and Union soldiers buried there. Also in 1866, memorial services were held at Antietam, the scene of the bloodiest one-day battle of the Civil War. Two years later, in 1868, General John A. Logan ordered that the graves of fallen Civil War soldiers be decorated. Apparently, a German-born soldier had told Logan about the German practice of decorating soldiers' graves each March 12 — a day the Germans called Heroes' Memorial Day.

During the early 1900s, nearly every city and small town throughout the United States held special Memorial Day programs. Civil War veterans would appear in their uniforms, and the day was filled with lengthy speeches, patriotic songs, and colorful parades. It was a day when everyone felt proud to be an American.

Today, Memorial Day is a much quieter holiday. Many citizens observe the day by flying the American flag over their homes. Some families visit cemeteries to place flowers on the graves of their loved ones. Yet some of the festive quality of the early celebrations lingers on. There are still parades, usually organized by veterans and armed forces organizations. The parades often feature local bands, Boy Scouts, Girl Scouts, and schoolchildren.

Some parts of the United States hold special events on Memorial Day. In Honolulu, Hawaii, schoolchildren weave flower *leis* each May to place on the graves of the Americans who died on the Hawaiian Islands during World War II. In Depoe, Oregon, a flotilla of private boats joins Coast Guard vessels in a "Fleet of Flowers" to honor the thousands of people who have died at sea. Passengers aboard the boats toss flowers into the water.

In Rindge, New Hampshire, a quiet ceremony takes place each year deep in a pine forest. On Memorial Day, the governor of each of the fifty states sends one white rose to the open-air cathedral at Rindge. Although the cathedral was built to honor a veteran of World War II, the U.S. Congress has recognized it as a memorial to all American war dead.

Memorial Day

Each statement below is either true or false. Circle the number of each true statement. Then, in the grid on the next page, shade in all the boxes that have the numbers you circled.

When you're finished, you'll complete another interesting fact about Memorial Day.

1. Memorial Day was originally a day to honor just those who died serving their country.

2. The idea of a day to honor the dead is very new.

3. Memorial Day in the United States started in 1966.

4. Waterloo, New York is known as the "Birthplace of Memorial Day."

5. Henry C. Welles suggested decorating the graves of Civil War dead.

6. In 1866, the women of Columbus, Mississippi honored only the Confederate soldiers buried in their cemetery.

7. Memorial services were held at Antietam, where many soldiers lost their lives during the Civil War.

8. General Logan came up with the idea for decorating soldiers' graves all by himself.

9. The Germans decorated soldiers' graves on their Heroes' Memorial Day.

10. Everyone ignored Memorial Day during the early 1900s.

11. Many U.S. citizens fly the flag on Memorial Day.

12. Some families visit cemeteries on Memorial Day.

13. In Hawaii, schoolchildren honor those who lost their lives during World War II.

14. Depoe, Oregon holds a ceremony to remember those who died in traffic accidents.

15. In Massachusetts, a quiet ceremony takes place each Memorial Day in a pine forest.

16. The governor of each of the fifty states sends a rose to Rindge, New Hampshire each Memorial Day.

On Memorial Day, many Boy Scouts and Girl Scouts visit veterans' cemeteries and on each grave place a tiny

13	11	4	2	12	2	10	8	12	5	11	9	8	4	11	16	7
16	2	3	8	7	6	2	14	7	3	6	1	2	13	3	8	2
1	9	12	14	4	3	15	3	13	16	5	7	10	12	6	1	13
5	15	2	10	9	2	6	2	1	14	2	4	15	16	10	2	7
4	3	8	6	5	16	12	10	9	15	10	12	3	5	13	9	12

Flag Day

If you seem to see a flag everywhere you turn, it's probably June 14 — Flag Day.

No one knows for sure just who created the very first American flag. In 1870, a grandson of Betsy Ross claimed that his grandmother sewed the first one under the direction of George Washington. While that story may not be true, Betsy Ross's home in Philadelphia is a national monument. Flag Day ceremonies often take place there.

The Bennington Flag is probably the oldest Stars & Stripes still around. It was carried into the Battle of Bennington in August 1777, during the American War for Independence. Today, this flag is on exhibit in Bennington, Vermont, honoring the two thousand Green Mountain Boys who defeated the British outside the town.

The Stars & Stripes took on a number of different patterns in the years that followed the winning of American independence. When Vermont and Kentucky joined the original thirteen states, the flag gained a new star and a new stripe for each of the new states. It was the flag with fifteen stars and stripes that was flying during the War of 1812 when Francis Scott Key wrote the words of "The Star Spangled Banner."

While Key, a lawyer, was visiting a prisoner on a British ship anchored in the Chesapeake Bay near the city of Baltimore, the British began bombarding Baltimore's Fort McHenry with cannonfire. Throughout the long night of September 13-14, 1814, Key remained on the deck of the ship, straining to see if the American flag still flew over Fort McHenry. Finally, by the light of the early dawn, he spotted it. He knew that his city of Baltimore had not fallen to the British. The same flag — ragged and bullet-torn — that inspired Francis Scott Key to write "The Star Spangled Banner" is on display at the Smithsonian Institution in Washington, D.C.

By 1818, more states were ready to join the Union. Congress decided, however, in the Flag Act to return to thirteen stripes and to add only new stars as the country added new states. That's why the flag we fly today has fifty stars — one for each of the fifty states — but only the thirteen original stripes.

It was in 1824 that the American flag was first called "Old Glory." In 1892 the Pledge of Allegiance was written, but it wasn't until 1954 that it included all the words recited today. Similarly, Flag Day goes all the way back to 1877, but it has been an official U.S. holiday only since 1949.

Probably the most colorful and interesting Flag Day celebration takes place each year in Fort Niagara State Park, New York. The French built Old Fort Niagara, which was occupied for a time by the British before the Americans took it over. On Flag Day, the French, British, and American flags all fly there while bands parade and play the national anthems of the three countries.

Flag Day

Use an encyclopedia or other reference book to find pictures of the flags identified below. Each one played a role in America's history. Draw each flag in the space provided, and then write a few facts about it on the lines at the right.

Bennington Flag, 1777

Fifteen Stars & Stripes, 1794-1818

American Flag of Your Choice

Flag Day

The time line at the right lists some of the important dates associated with the American flag. Identify the event that goes with each date. The first one is done for you.

Bennington flag carried into battle _____	1777
_____	1814
_____	1818
_____	1824
_____	1870
_____	1877
_____	1892
_____	1949
_____	1954

Father's Day

People in the United States celebrate Father's Day on the third Sunday in June. It's a happy time for family gatherings and giving gifts to dear ol' Dad.

A special day to remember and honor fathers goes all the way back to ancient Rome. Every February, the Romans held a ten-day festival called *"Parentalia."* During *Parentalia,* families would honor fathers and other relatives who were no longer living. They would decorate the graves of their dead kin with wine, milk, honey, oil, water, and flowers. Actually, the holiday turned into an annual reunion, with everyone returning home from the graveyard to a big family feast.

The first known Father's Day service in the United States took place in a church in Fairmont, West Virginia on July 5, 1908. That service, however, did not lead to a permanent Father's Day holiday. Instead, it was Mrs. John Bruce Dodd of Spokane, Washington who contributed the most to making Father's Day a U.S. holiday.

Although many people claim to have been the first to suggest a Father's Day celebration in the United States, it was Mrs. Dodd who really put the idea into practice. While listening to a sermon on Mother's Day in 1909, Mrs. Dodd began to think of all her father had done for her and for her five brothers. By 1910, she had convinced the city of Spokane to issue the first Father's Day proclamation, and it became the first U.S. city to honor fathers. Mrs. Dodd suggested the rose as the flower for the day — a red rose for a father who was still living and a white rose for a father who had died. She also suggested that the family attend church and give a small gift to father on Father's Day.

In 1924, President Calvin Coolidge asked that Father's Day be observed in all parts of the United States. It took until 1972, however, for Father's Day to become a permanent holiday in this country.

Today, more than twenty countries around the world honor fathers with a special day. Canadians celebrate the holiday on the same Sunday in June as do the people of the United States. In Australia, the holiday falls on the first Sunday in September, while in New Zealand, Father's Day takes place on the second Sunday in September. In Norway, fathers get a whole month — November — of special attention each year!

Father's Day

Each statement below is either true or false. Circle the number of every true statement. Then, in the grid on the next page, shade in all the boxes that have the numbers you circled.

When you're finished, you'll see the name of the most important person on Father's Day.

1. Father's Day always falls on June 3.

2. In 1972, Father's Day became a permanent holiday in the United States.

3. The Greeks held a festival called *Parentalia*.

4. On *Parentalia*, families honored fathers and other relatives who were no longer living.

5. Families decorated the graves of relatives on *Parentalia*.

6. The first U.S. Father's Day services took place in West Virginia.

7. Mrs. John Bruce Dodd contributed most to making Father's Day a U.S. holiday.

8. Mrs. Dodd lived in Seattle, Washington.

9. Mrs. Dodd got the idea for Father's Day on Mother's Day.

10. Mrs. Dodd appreciated all that her father had done for her and her brothers.

11. Spokane, Washington was the first U.S. city to honor fathers.

12. It was Mrs. Dodd's brother who chose the rose as the flower for Father's Day.

13. A red rose was supposed to honor a father who had died.

14. Mrs. Dodd suggested that people attend church on Father's Day.

15. President Calvin Coolidge made Father's Day a national holiday.

16. More than twenty countries around the world have a special day to honor fathers.

2	16	4	9	13	8	4	11	16	9	1	8	16	5	14	10
1	9	8	6	3	12	10	15	8	6	13	1	12	11	8	16
3	10	1	2	15	1	5	14	4	2	3	15	3	9	1	4
15	5	3	4	12	13	11	13	12	7	8	12	13	14	12	7
14	7	11	14	15	3	14	15	8	16	15	8	10	6	9	6

Midsummer And St. John's Day

In Europe, people have been celebrating Midsummer Day on June 24 for many centuries. Much of the celebrating centers around a bonfire. Early sun-worshippers probably built fires to symbolize the sun's life-giving warmth and light. They would dance around and leap over the flames, believing that their bonfires had magical powers to cure the sick and drive away the witches that flew about on Midsummer's Eve.

As the years passed, sun-worshipping disappeared and Midsummer Day became a holiday for young lovers. On Midsummer Day, young men and women were supposed to discover the identity of the person they would fall in love with and marry. When Christians began to observe June 24 as the birthday of Saint John the Baptist, many Midsummer customs were transferred to the new holiday — St. John's Day.

In many European countries today, the bonfires (sometimes called St. John's fires) are still part of the celebration. Holiday fires blaze atop hills, besides lakes, and along the seacoasts. In cities and towns, bonfires light up the streets, and in some places people still jump over the flames. English and Austrian couples throw flowers into the fire and then jump over it, hoping that they will soon marry. French children leap high over the fires, believing that the crops will grow as high as they jump.

In the Russian countryside, children dance around bonfires and tell each other stories about a magical fern that appears once a year. At midnight, they search the woods for the fern, believing that if they find it they will have good luck all their lives.

In parts of France, people throw burning torches high in the air instead of lighting bonfires. They also set fire to straw-covered wheels and then roll the wheels down hills. Wheels that keep burning until they reach the bottom of the hill are a sign of good luck. Out at sea, French fishermen celebrate the holiday by stuffing a barrel with old clothing, raising the barrel high on the main mast, and then setting it afire. What a sight it is to see when all the ships in a fishing fleet have flames shooting skyward from their masts!

In South America they call the holiday *El Dia de San Juan,* and it's a time for singing and dancing. It's also a time for eating and drinking. At the *fiesta* (party), people roast sweet potatoes and green corn over a fire. The adults enjoy a special drink called *quentao,* made of sugar cane, brandy, lemon, and spices.

In Brazil, family members named John prepare a bonfire and invite relatives and friends to take part in the holiday celebration. In Puerto Rico, families have a picnic at the beach from midnight to dawn on Midsummer's Eve. They sing and eat as they sit around a bonfire. They also wade in the warm waters of the Caribbean. The custom of wading in water may have begun in connection with St. John's baptism of Jesus.

In many countries, fortune-telling is a popular part of the holiday. Some people believe that an egg broken in a glass of water at night can predict the future. The design formed by the white of the egg when looked at the following morning is supposed to reveal a person's fortune. Unmarried girls try to find out whom they will marry on the holiday. They write the names of their boyfriends on pieces of paper. Then they toss aside the pieces one by one. The last remaining piece of paper is supposed to have the name of each girl's future husband.

Midsummer is especially popular in the Scandinavian countries. In Sweden, people celebrate by adorning doorways, balconies, boats, and cars with natural greenery: newly cut birch trees, leaves, and branches. Almost every village puts up a *najstang* — a spruce trunk that is wound with garlands something like a maypole.

In Norway, schools close so that everyone can go to picnics along the fjords. Bonfires blaze close to the glistening water. Boats decorated with flowers and green branches float nearby so that their passengers can get a good view of the bonfires. The Danes use their bonfires to burn effigies of witches, while the Finns combine Midsummer with the celebration of their Flag Day. All over Scandinavia, people dress in traditional costumes on the holiday.

In the United States, people of Scandinavian descent celebrate Midsummer, too. For example, the Danish community in Ephraim, Wisconsin welcomes summer by burning straw witches. In Minneapolis and St. Paul, Minnesota, many people attend religious services, folk dances, concerts, and picnics on June 24. In northern Alaska, people celebrate Midsummer as the midnight sun. Since there is no real night in Alaska at the summer solstice, children stay up from evening to morning with their parents. Everyone celebrates through the twilight hours by eating, playing games, and dancing.

Midsummer And St. John's Day

Complete each sentence below by unscrambling the letters in the missing word or words. But beware! Each set of scrambled letters contains an extra letter. In the first sentence, for example, "r f n g e" spells "fern" with a "g" left over.

As you unscramble the missing words, put the extra letters on the blanks at the bottom of the next page. Be sure to match the number of the sentence with the number of the blank for each extra letter.

When you're finished, you'll find that the extra letters spell a special holiday wish for you.

1. Russian children tell stories about a magical _____fern (+g)_____ that appears once a year. r f n g e

2. Midsummer takes place on _____ 24. o J e u n

3. Bonfires are sometimes called _____. t. S n' J h o s   i o f r e s

4. Early sun-worshippers most likely built bonfires to symbolize the power of the sun's warmth and

   _____. g l d t i h

5. In Sweden, people decorate houses, boats, and cars with branches and green _____.
   l l e e v a s

6. In northern Alaska, Midsummer Day is a celebration of the _____ _____.
   n t m d i i h g   u n s u

7. Many _____ _____ _____ customs come from Midsummer
   Day celebrations. S c t. s J o n' h   a D y

8. A long time ago, people thought bonfires had _____ powers. g a k l m c a i

9. In France, straw-covered wagon wheels that keep burning are supposed to bring good

   _____. k t u l c

10. In Sweden, there is a _____ welcome for Midsummer. o e e r n g

11. The _____ in Norway are aglow with bonfires. j y d f r o s

12. In Brazil, family members named _____ make the holiday bonfires. o J o n h

13. In South America, St. John's Day is called *El Dia de* _____ _____.
    a S n   n u u J a

14. On Midsummer's Eve in Puerto Rico, people _____ in the water. a d w e a

15. The people of Finland combine the Midsummer celebration with their _____
    _____. g l F a   l y D a

16. Some people try to find out whom they will _____ during the Midsummer celebration.
    w m y r a r

17. In Scandinavia, people wear traditional _____. t c a o e s s m u

18. Some people in France toss burning _____ instead of lighting bonfires. h o c y e t r s

19. Swedish villages put up something like a _____. p s m l a e o y

The Fortune-Telling Egg's Secret Holiday Message:

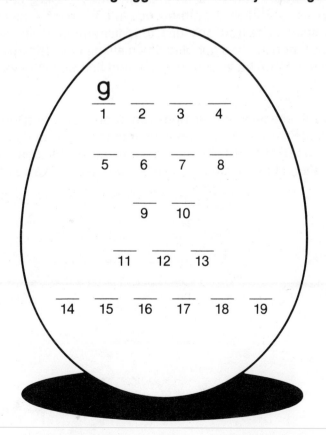

g
1 2 3 4

5 6 7 8

9 10

11 12 13

14 15 16 17 18 19

Dragon Boat Festival

The Dragon Boat Festival, celebrated in China each year on June 24, is also known as *Dyun Ngn Jit.* On this holiday, the Chinese people re-enact the search for the body of Ch'u Yuan. Ch'u Yuan, a well-known statesman and poet, felt that his government was unjust to the Chinese people. He believed that to see a wrong and not try to right it was evil.

In trying to help his people, Ch'u Yuan angered an important prince. The prince accused Ch'u Yuan of being dishonorable. Since Ch'u Yuan was a common man, he could not defend himself against a prince. He grew very unhappy, and on the fifth day of the fifth moon he drowned himself in the Mi-Lo River in Hunan province. The year was 403 B.C.

When people heard what Ch'u Yuan had done, they rushed to the river to save him. Each one wanted to be the first to offer him rice and sweets. They decorated their boats with flags, and they sounded gongs to keep away evil spirits. But they were too late to help Ch'u Yuan.

The Chinese people wanted to honor the memory of this great statesman and poet. To keep his spirit alive, they threw rice into the river. According to legend, Ch'u Yuan's spirit appeared one day to a fisherman. The spirit said that a dragon-like sea monster had gobbled down all the rice. The spirit of Ch'u Yuan suggested that the rice be wrapped in silk and tied up with five silk threads of different colors.

Today, the Chinese people wrap rice in bamboo leaves and tie it with string for the Dragon Boat Festival. They dress in their best clothes and meet at rivers and lakes to watch boat races. The boats, long and narrow and shaped like dragons, re-enact the efforts to save Ch'u Yuan's life and to chase away the rice-eating dragon.

Dragon Boat Festival

Unscramble the letters to find the missing word or words in each sentence below. But beware! Each set of scrambled letters contains an extra letter.

   For example, in the first sentence, "n f C i h a" spells "China" with an "f" left over. As you complete each sentence, enter the extra letter — in order — on the blanks at the bottom of the next page. When you're finished, you'll find that the extra letters spell another name for the Dragon Boat Festival.

1. The Dragon Boat Festival takes place in ___China (+f)___.
   nfCiha

2. The Dragon Boat Festival is also known as

   _____ _____ _____.
   enDyu   nNg   tiJ

3. On Dragon Boat Day, the Chinese re-enact the search for the body of

   _____ _____.
   uCh'   Ysnau

4. Ch'u Yuan drowned in the _____ River.
   iM-Lto

5. Ch'u Yuan was a _____ as well as an honest statesman.
   tiope

6. Ch'u Yuan felt his government was _____ to the people.
   jnuuvts

7. Ch'u Yuan angered an important _____.
   renpica

8. Ch'u Yuan was accused of being _____.
   binoldsrohael

9. When he could not prove his good intentions, Ch'u Yuan was _____.
   ppuaonhy

10. On the fifth day of the fifth _____, Ch'u Yuan threw himself in the river.
    n f o m o

11. Ch'u Yuan died in _____ province.
    n u t n H a

12. When people heard that Ch'u Yuan had thrown himself into the river, they raced after him in their

    _____.
    s h o t a b

13. People decorated their boats and sounded _____ to drive away evil spirits.
    o e s g n g

14. The Chinese decided to _____ Ch'u Yuan's memory because he was a great man.
    h h r o o n

15. People threw _____ in the river to keep Ch'u Yuan's ghost alive.
    c i i r e

16. A_____ _____ was supposed to have eaten the food thrown into the river
    e s a   e s g r m t o n
    for Ch'u Yuan.

17. According to legend, Ch'u Yuan's spirit suggested that the rice be wrapped in _____ to
    protect it.   i k l h s

18. On Dragon Boat Day, there are races of boats shaped like _____.
    n a s r o d n g

19. The Dragon Boat races re-enact the efforts to _____ Ch'u Yuan.
    s e v a o

20. According to legend, Ch'u Yuan's spirit appeared one day to a _____.
    h s m f n e o i r a

21. The Dragon Boat Festival is celebrated on June _____ _____.
    t t n e y w   t n u h o f r

Another name for the Dragon Boat Festival is

f __ __ __ __ __ __ __ __ __ __ __ __ __
1 2 3 4 5 6 7 8 9 10 11 12 13

__ __ __ __ __ __ __ __
14 15 16 17 18 19 20 21

198

Dominion Day

Dominion Day on July 1 celebrates the creation of the country of Canada in 1867. It's a day for fireworks and parades, just like the U.S. Independence Day festivities. In fact, because the holidays come so close together, the two neighboring countries hold a joint celebration in cities just across the border from each other.

The celebration is called the International Freedom Festival, and it salutes both Dominion Day and the Fourth of July. It takes place in the cities of Detroit, Michigan and Windsor, Ontario. The festivities include a gold cup powerboat race, baton-twirling and kite-flying contests, sky-diving exhibitions, a pleasure craft water parade, an art exhibit, puppet shows, concerts, and an old-fashioned hootenany.

The story of Canada and of Dominion Day begins with the coming of the European explorers to the New World. John Cabot reached the Canadian coast off Newfoundland in 1497. In 1535, Jacques Cartier led a French expedition up the Saint Lawrence River. In the 1600s, both France and England sent explorers and trappers into Canada. Europeans liked fur hats at the time, and there were great profits to be made from the trade in Canadian beaver skins.

In the 1700s, France and England fought a series of wars. The Seven Years' War (1757-1763) ended with the English winning all of Canada. But the French settlers — living mostly in Quebec — were allowed to keep their language, religion, and customs. Canada is still a bicultural country.

On July 1, 1867, the four original Canadian provinces — Quebec, Ontario, Nova Scotia, and New Brunswick — formed the Dominion of Canada. A few years later, when Manitoba, Prince Edward Island, and British Columbia joined the Dominion, the Canadian provinces stretched from sea to sea. Unlike their U.S. neighbors to the south, the Canadians didn't have to fight a war with England to gain their freedom. The British Parliament passed a bill that allowed Canada to govern itself.

During the twentieth century, three more provinces have joined the Dominion. Alberta and Saskatchewan joined in 1905, with Newfoundland (including Labrador) joining in 1948. Canada also has two territories: the Northwest and the Yukon.

Dominion Day

How well do you know Canada? Use an atlas to help you complete the map of Canada below.

1. Label the four original provinces, and color them green.

2. Label the next three provinces to join the Dominion, and color them orange.

3. Label the two provinces that joined the Dominion in 1905, and color them yellow.

4. Label the most recent Canadian province, and color it red.

5. Label the two Canadian territories, and color them brown.

6. Draw a star on the site of the annual International Freedom Festival.

You'll find a picture of Canada's flag in an encyclopedia. Use the space below to draw and color the flag. Be sure to use the correct colors.

July 4, 1776

The Fourth of July has been an American holiday for more than two hundred years. The events leading up to the first Fourth of July celebration began in 1607. In that year, a small group of settlers founded the first permanent English colony in America at Jamestown, Virginia. Eventually, thirteen colonies dotted the Atlantic coastline. All the colonies were under the rule of the King of England.

Until the 1760s, however, England didn't pay much attention to its American colonies. Then England decided to tax the colonists. Americans were forced to pay taxes on tea, glass, paper, and other items they needed. Many refused to buy these taxed items, and some began to talk about wanting more power to govern themselves.

In December 1773, some Boston colonists dressed as Indians slipped aboard an English ship docked in the harbor. During the dark winter night, the "Indians" dumped the ship's cargo of tea overboard into the water. This protest against British policies became known as the "Boston Tea Party."

The British Parliament was furious and decided to punish the Bostonians. British troops were stationed in Boston, and many were housed in private homes. Public meetings were outlawed, and the Port of Boston was closed.

In September 1774, the First Continental Congress met in Philadelphia. The colonists who attended the Congress were angry and unhappy about British policies. But they still thought of themselves as loyal to England. They drew up a Declaration of Rights, hoping that the British Parliament would change its policies toward the American colonies. The British would not change.

By April 1775, fighting between Britain and her American colonies was close at hand. And with the battles at Lexington and Concord that month, America's War for Independence began. In June 1776, the Second Continental Congress appointed a committee to draft a Declaration of Independence.

One member of the committee, Thomas Jefferson, wrote most of the Declaration of Independence. In the preamble he wrote that "all men are created equal" and that they have a right to "life, liberty, and the pursuit of happiness." The second part of the Declaration listed twenty-eight wrongs committed by the King of England against the colonies. And the third part resolved that the American colonies should be and were independent states.

On July 4, 1776, the Continental Congress approved the Declaration of Independence. John Hancock, president of the Congress, signed his name at the bottom in huge letters. He wanted to make sure the King of England could read it without his glasses! But it was an act of bravery for all the Americans to sign the Declaration of Independence. Had the United States lost its war with England, all who signed would have surely faced the death sentence as traitors.

Outside the State House in Philadelphia (later renamed Independence Hall), an eager crowd gathered, waiting to hear whether the Congress would vote for independence. When they heard the decision, the Philadelphians went wild with excitement. As the news spread, Americans everywhere celebrated with huge bonfires and other festivities. Ever since that day in 1776, the Fourth of July has been a time for Americans to celebrate their freedom.

Today, the original Declaration of Independence is housed in the National Archives in Washington, D.C. The Liberty Bell, which rang out the news of independence from the top of the State House, is on display at Independence Hall in Philadelphia.

July 4, 1776

The pieces below form a picture familiar to all Americans. Cut out the picture pieces, and then arrange them from top to bottom in the order in which the events happened. In other words, the top piece should be the earliest event, and the bottom piece should be the last event.

When you have all the pieces in the correct order, paste them on a separate sheet of paper.

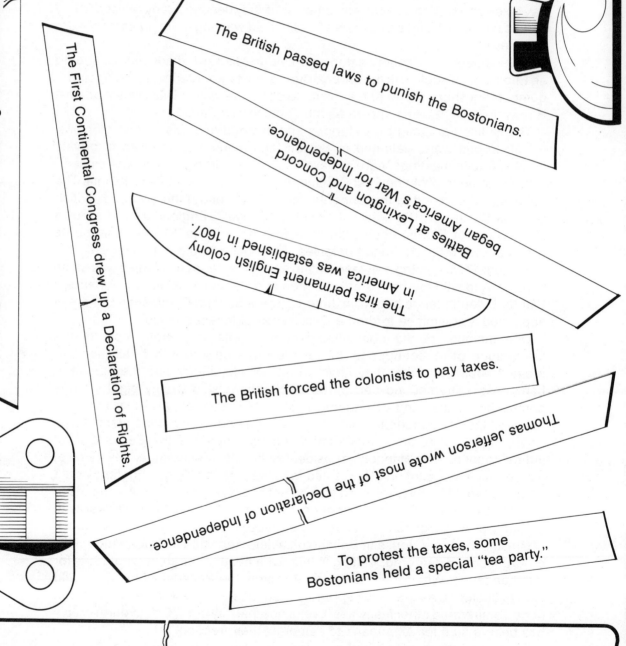

Delegates from all the colonies signed the Declaration of Independence.

The First Continental Congress drew up a Declaration of Rights.

The British passed laws to punish the Bostonians.

Battles at Lexington and Concord began America's War for Independence.

The first permanent English colony in America was established in 1607.

The British forced the colonists to pay taxes.

Thomas Jefferson wrote most of the Declaration of Independence.

To protest the taxes, some Bostonians held a special "tea party."

The United States won its independence.

Fourth of July Celebrations

July 4 is the biggest summer holiday throughout the United States. The day is filled with family picnics, parades, and sporting events, while the night is a time for brilliant fireworks displays.

On July 4, 1777 — a year after the Declaration of Independence was signed in their city — Philadelphians celebrated with bonfires, fireworks, and thirteen-gun salutes from ships anchored in the harbor. Eleven years later, on July 4, 1788, Philadelphia cheered the adoption of the United States Constitution with a three-hour parade that stretched out for more than a mile.

In 1876, to honor America's one-hundredth birthday, Philadelphia once again led the celebrations. The city hosted a world's fair that attracted almost ten million visitors (about one-fifth of the U.S. population at the time). Exhibits came from thirty-nine countries. England, France, and Italy loaned art treasures for the celebration. But sculptor Frederic Bartholdi was unable to complete a special gift from France in time for the fair. Eight years later, the French gift — the monument we call the Statue of Liberty — stood complete in New York Harbor. In 1876, however, the only part of the statue that could be displayed at the fair was the lady's hand.

For the nation's two-hundredth birthday on July 4, 1976, Americans joined in a celebration called the Bicentennial. Bells sounded all around the country at the same hour in the afternoon. There were parades, concerts, re-enactments of historical events — and, of course, fireworks. New York staged a gigantic "Operation Sail" for the Bicentennial. A rare collection of sixteen tall-masted ships joined hundreds of other sailing vessels from many lands in a procession up and down the Hudson River. In Philadelphia, more than one million visitors had a chance to see an outdoor display of the famous Liberty Bell.

Some towns and cities conduct special July 4 celebrations every year. The small Pennsylvania town of Lititz, for example, holds a Festival of Candles. The people of the town arrange thousands of candles in star, wheel, and pyramid shapes. Then they light the candles and set their creations floating on a nearby lake.

In Hannibal, Missouri — the hometown of Mark Twain — young people compete in an annual National Fence Painting Contest that would surely delight the heart of Tom Sawyer. In Bristol, Rhode Island, fire engine companies from all over New England gather to take part in a water-squirting competition. It is Ontario, California, however, that boasts the biggest July 4 picnic in the United States. Tables stretch down the middle of one of the city's streets for a distance of two miles!

Fourth Of July Celebrations

Have you ever wanted to work on a newspaper? Here is your chance! Imagine that you are the news reporter assigned to cover the events that match the datelines below. Write a good lead sentence for each dateline, including all the main facts: who, what, when, where, and how. The first one is done for you.

Philadelphia, PA, July 4, 1777:   Philadelphians today celebrated the first anniversary of the signing of the Declaration of Independence with bonfires, fireworks, and thirteen-gun salutes.

Philadelphia, PA, July 4, 1876: _____

_____

_____

New York City, July 4, 1976: _____

_____

_____

Bristol, Rhode Island, July 4, 198___: _____

_____

_____

Hannibal, Missouri, July 4, 198___: _____

_____

_____

Lititz, PA, July 4, 198___: _____

_____

_____

Ontario, CA, July 4, 198___: _____

_____

_____

Every newspaper also has feature reporters. While these reporters must include the who/what/when/where/how facts, they emphasize "human interest" in their stories. They try to describe what the people involved in the story are doing, saying, and thinking.

Use your imagination and what you now know about Fourth of July celebrations to write a feature story for one of the datelines.

_____

_____

_____

_____

_____

_____

_____

_____

_____

_____

_____

_____

_____

Bastille Day

Flags of red, white, and blue wave in the breeze. Fireworks explode in the night sky. Families gather to celebrate a holiday of freedom. No, it is not July 4 —Independence Day — in the United States of America. It is July 14 in France, Bastille Day.

Back in 1789, the French people had been ruled by kings for centuries, and some of them thought that the time had come for the people to rule themselves. The American people had been governing themselves ever since declaring their independence in 1776. America's Declaration of Independence was very popular in France.

On July 14, 1789, an angry mob attacked the Bastille, a huge jail in Paris, where many men and women had been imprisoned. The fortress fell to the mob, and the prisoners were set free. King Louis XVI stayed in power for a few more years, but he was later put to death on the *guillotine.*

The fall of the Bastille marked the beginning of the French Revolution. The cry of the Revolution was *"Liberté, Egalité, Fraternité"* (Liberty, Equality, Fraternity). Many of the ideas behind the Revolution were put into a document called the Declaration of the Rights of Man. Many of those ideas also appeared in the American Declaration of Independence and the Bill of Rights.

Unlike the people of the United States, the French had to wait a hundred years for their country to have a stable democracy. Nevertheless, they still celebrate July 14 as the day they began their movement toward representative government and the protection of their rights.

Each Bastille Day, a great military parade marches down the Champs-Elysees in Paris, one of the widest streets in the world. The famous *Garde Republicaine* are at the front of the parade, riding shiny black horses and wearing uniforms of scarlet, black, and white. Paratroopers and naval cadets follow, while bands fill the air with the music of the *Marseillaise,* the French national anthem. The marchers proudly salute the red, white, and blue flag of France at the Arch of Triumph. And low-flying jets climax the parade by trailing streams of red, white, and blue smoke.

After the main parade, Parisians hold smaller neighborhood parades throughout the city to celebrate Bastille Day. It's also a day for block parties, with music and dancing in the streets.

Name_____

Bastille Day

Complete each statement below by filling in the missing word or words. Then find the words and circle them in the word-search puzzle. You'll have to look carefully. The words in the puzzle may be spelled in any direction — even backwards.

After you find all the words in the puzzle, put the extra letters — in order — on the blanks at the bottom of the next page. You'll see that the extra letters spell out the answers to two mystery questions.

1. The French began their fight for self-government on July

____ ____ ____ ____ ____ ____ ____ ____ ____.

2. This day became known as ____ ____ ____ ____ ____ ____ ____ ____ Day.

3. Americans declared their freedom on July ____ ____ ____ ____ ____ ____.

4. This day is known as ____ ____ ____ ____ ____ ____ ____ ____ ____ ____ ____ Day.

5. For many years, the French people had been ruled by a ____ ____ ____ ____.

6. The Americans were ruled by the King of ____ ____ ____ ____ ____ ____ ____.

7. The French wrote the Declaration of the ____ ____ ____ ____ ____ ____ of ____ ____ ____.

8. Many of the French ideas also appeared in America's

____ ____ ____ ____ ____ ____ ____ ____ ____ ____ ____ of Independence and

____ ____ ____ ____ of Rights.

9. America declared its independence in seventeen seventy ____ ____ ____.

10. France did not achieve a stable democracy for another one

____ ____ ____ ____ ____ ____ ____ years.

11. The famous cry of the French Revolution was " ____ ____ ____ ____ ____ ____ ____,

____ ____ ____ ____ ____ ____ ____,

____ ____ ____ ____ ____ ____ ____!"

g	i	v	e	r	i	g	h	t	s	m	e
i	n	d	e	p	e	n	d	e	n	c	e
l	o	e	i	b	f	e	r	t	k	y	t
o	i	t	n	r	g	o	i	v	i	e	i
m	t	r	a	g	e	d	u	e	n	a	n
t	a	e	m	h	l	p	a	r	g	t	r
r	r	b	i	e	g	a	l	i	t	e	e
c	a	i	b	k	h	e	n	n	r	h	t
e	l	l	i	t	s	a	b	d	y	o	a
s	c	f	l	v	i	r	g	i	n	i	r
i	e	a	l	h	u	n	d	r	e	d	f
x	d	f	o	u	r	t	e	e	n	t	h

Mystery Questions:

What was the famous cry before the American War for Independence?

— — — — — — — — — — — — — —

— — — — — — — — — — — !

Who said it?

— — — — — — — — — — —

— — — — — — — —

Answer Key

Labor Day
True Statements: 1, 2, 4, 6, 7, 10, 14, 15, 18, 19

— 5 —

The Ramadan Fast And Id-Ul-Fitr
1. p 2. a. 3. i 4. n 5. t 6. c 7. o 8. l 9. o 10. r 11. r 12. a 13. i 14. n 15. b 16. o 17. w 18. d 19. r 20. e 21. s 22. s
Children paint their pets every color in the rainbow to dress them up.

— 7 —

Mid-Autumn Festival/Tĕt-Trung-Thu
1. What is another name for the Mid-Autumn Festival?
2. Who dreamed that he visited the moon?
3. What special treat do Vietnamese children and adults enjoy during the Mid-Autumn Festival?
4. On what do the people of Vietnam base their calendar?
5. Around what date does the Mid-Autumn Festival usually fall?
6. What do Vietnamese boys and girls build in the shapes of rabbits, fish, birds, etc.?
7. As they swing their lamps on festival night, where do the children imagine they are going?
8. What do children do on festival night?
9. What do parents use to mold tiny animal shapes for their children?
10. What do teenagers and adults do while gazing at the bright moon?
11. What have the Vietnamese had ever since the days of Emperor Minh-Mang?
12. What shape are moon cakes?

— 12 —

American Indian Day
Cochise
  Tribe: Apache
  Where the tribe lived: Southwest
  Why Cochise began to fight: He was arrested for something he did not do.
Geronimo
  Tribe: Apache
  Where the tribe lived: Southwest
  Why Geronimo began to fight: First, the killing of his family; later, the betrayal of his people.
Chief Joseph
  Tribe: Nez Percé
  Where the tribe lived: Oregon
  Why Chief Joseph began to fight: He had no choice when his warriors killed settlers.

```
1.            t  r  i  b  e
              e
2.  p  r  o  m  i  s  e
              e
3.            f  r  i  e  n  d
              v
4.         f  e  a  r
              t
5.            f  i  g  h  t
              o
6.         l  a  n  d
```

— 15 —

Chusongnal
1. The Korean day of thanksgiving is in September.
2. People honor their ancestors.
3. Children give a bow to their parents.
4. People give thanks for a good harvest.
5. Each family member sits around a low table.
6. Every year a farmers' band plays.
7. Rice cakes are in the shape of a half moon.
8. In Korea, *kimchee* is a special treat.
9. Friends exchange gifts of food on this day.
10. Music and dancing are part of *Chusongnal*.
The people give thanks each year in Korea on *Chusongnal*.

Rosh Hashanah And Yom Kippur
1. celebrated 2. harvest 3. began 4. middle 5. *Rosh Hashanah* 6. wrongdoings 7. *Yom Kippur* 8. sundown 9. thoughtful
10. *shofar* 11. fast 12. *tsimmes* 13. wish 14. Life 15. year 16. deeds 17. *hallah* 18. future
Rosh Hashanah means beginning of the year.

--- **20** ---

Oktoberfest
1. U 2. T 3. B 4. E 5. O 6. K 7. R 8. O 9. F 10. N
Oktoberfest has just begun.
It's time to have
Oktober fun!

--- **22** ---

Christopher Columbus
1. T 2. F 3. F 4. T 5. F 6. T 7. F 8. F 9. T 10. T 11. F 12. T 13. F 14. F 15. T 16. T 17. F 18. F 19. T 20. T 21. T
22. F 23. F 24. F 25. T 26. T 27. T 28. F 29. F 30. T 31. F 32. T 33. T 34. F 35. F

--- **26** ---

Columbus Day Celebrations
1. parade 2. President 3. statue 4. construction 5. events 6. New York - Maryland 7. Italy 8. Barcelona 9. pageant 10. sixteen
11. federal 12. San Francisco 13. hundred 14. flag
The two other names for Columbus Day are: discovery day and landing day.

--- **29** ---

West African Harvest Festivals
1. r 2. s 3. i 4. l 5. a 6. h 7. v 8. e 9. n 10. f 11. t
Harvest Rhyme:
if rains fall,
the harvest's tall

--- **31** ---

Halloween History
1. T 2. F 3. T 4. T 5. F 6. T 7. T 8. F 9. T 10. T 11. F 12. T 13. T 14. F 15. T 16. T 17. T 18. F 19. T 20. T 21. F 22. T
23. T 24. T 25. F 26. F 27. T 28. T 29. F 30. T 31. T 32. T 33. F 34. F 35. T 36. T 37. T 38. T 39. F 40. F 41. T 42. T
43. T 44. T 45. F 46. T 47. T 48. F 49. T 50. T

--- **36** ---

Halloween Celebrations

Other names
for Halloween
were Nut Crack
Night and
Snap Apple
Night.

To many colonists
in America
witches and devils
seemed very real,
and Halloween was
not a night of fun.

When the Irish
came to the U.S.,
Halloween became
a very
popular American
holiday.

Long ago in Scotland,
people tried to
outdo one another
with the largest
and brightest
bonfires.

People in France
would put
pancakes and cider
on graves
to welcome
the dead.

When the fires
burned out,
early Scots
would run so
that the devil
wouldn't catch them.

American pioneers
enjoyed sitting
by the fire,
roasting nuts
and telling
ghost stories.

--- **39** ---

Halloween Customs And Superstitions
1. a 2. h 3. m 4. s 5. n 6. d 7. w 8. c 9. o 10. i 11. t 12. e 13. l 14. t
What does a witch love to eat on Halloween?
a ham sandwitch on whole wheat

--- **41** ---

El Dia De Los Muertos
1. first 2. honors 3. United States 4. All Souls' Day 5. dead 6. play 7. California 8. coffins 9. toy 10. human 11. *calaveras*
12. marigold 13. firecrackers 14. meal 15. holiday
The words "*El Dia De Los Muertos*" mean
the day of the dead

44

Diwali

True Statements: 2, 5, 6, 8, 11, 13, 15, 17, 18, 19, 20

— **49** —

Veterans Day

1. World 2. November 3. Armistice 4. soldiers 5. Cemetery 6. But 7. wreath 8. peace 9. veterans 10. silence 11. celebration

Canadians call Veterans Day
remembrance day

— **51** —

Shichi-Go-San

1. lucky 2. November 3. toddlers 4. babyhood 5. beginning 6. clothes 7. respect 8. shrines 9. trouble 10. worms 11. life 12. Relatives 13. *chitoseame* 14. *obi* 15. together 16. why 17. pleated 18. boys and girls 19. *Kamioki* 20. floss silk 21. bundle 22. thousand-year 23. *hakama* 24. little 25. women 26. symbol

Japanese children learn from their parents that love
is deeper than the sea and
higher than the mountains

— **54** —

Loy Krathong

True Statements: 1, 2, 4, 6, 7, 10, 12, 14
Similar Holiday: Diwali

— **57** —

Thanksgiving History

1. religious (+p) 2. Mayflower (+a) 3. Massachusetts (+t) 4. seeds (+h) 5. Sarah Hale (+w) 6. friendship (+f) 7. President (+s) Lincoln 8. Thanksgiving (+r) 9. Indians (+y) 10. date (+p) 11. grateful (+m) 12. Squanto (+k) 13. pumpkin (+v) 14. three (+i) 15. Popcorn (+d) 16. George Washington (+j) 17. survived (+z) 18. fourth (+l) 19. food (+m)

— **61** —

Thanksgiving Celebrations Through The Ages

1. food 2. thanksgiving 3. sharing 4. Martinmas 5. goddesses/grains/orchards 6. lanterns 7. Ceres 8. needy 9. festival/fruitfulness 10. parade/harvest wagon 11. Harvest Home 12. growing 13. Europe 14. St. Martin of Tours 15. kern maiden, corn doll, wreath, bird feeder

Turkeys suggest that you...
eat lots of ham
during thanksgiving time.

— **64** —

Lucia Day

1. legend 2. *Luciadagen* 3. processions 4. Sicily 5. pagan 6. harm 7. sword 8. solstice 9. daughter 10. white 11. light 12. village 13. candles 14. Lucia 15. sash 16. coffee 17. *lussekatter* 18. *St. Järngossar* 19. hospitals 20. season

What warning should the Lucia bride receive before putting on her crown?
Please candle with care!

— **67** —

Hanukkah History

1. f 2. e 3. s 4. t 5. i 6. v 7. a 8. l 9. o 10. f 11. l 12. i 13. g 14. h 15. t 16. s

Another name for Hanukkah is
Festival of lights

— **69** —

Hanukkah Celebrations

ACROSS: 3. presents 5. *latkes* 7. *menorah* 9. liberty 11. Antiochus 12. lamps 13. happy

DOWN: 1. *Gelt* 2. *dreidel* 4. relay 6. *shammash* 8. Tel Aviv 10. candle

— **72** —

Christmas Origins

In the small town of **Bethlehem**
A little Child was born,
Over **two** thousand years ago
On the first **Christmas** morn.

Mary wrapped Him in
swaddling clothes
And laid Him in a **manger.**
There was no room in any **inn**
For this little stranger.

In nearby fields were **shepherds**
Who watched their **flocks** by night.
They heard the **angel's** message
And hurried to the site.

Next came three **wise** men or Magi
Who traveled from afar.
They, too, found the Infant
By following a **star.**

— 74

Christmas Traditions
The first St. Nicholas was a kindly bishop of the fourth century.
The tradition of music goes back to the first Christmas.
Christmas trees were used in Germany in the 1500s.
St. Francis of Assisi had the idea for the first Nativity scene.
The first Christmas cards appeared in England in the 1840s.
Dutch sailors brought news of St. Nicholas to Holland.
Early gifts and ornaments were usually homemade.
Traveling actors performing Christmas plays inspired the custom of caroling.
Early carols were written in Italy.
Christmas trees were popular in America by the middle of the 19th century.

— 78

Christmas In Europe
1. Advent calendar; Germany   2. St. Nicholas arriving; Holland   3. *Christkindle;* Switzerland
4. Parents decorate tree; Germany, Austria, Poland, or England.   5. Dining table covered with straw; Serbia
6. Children asking for treats; Sweden   7. Candle in window for travelers; Ireland   8. Feed tree for birds; Austria   9. Coin baked in bread; Greec
10. Blindfolded children waiting for Christ Child; Italy

— 84

Christmas In Latin America
Nacimiento/Nativity Scene   Poinsettia/Native To Mexico   Colombia/Night of *Aguinaldos*   Peru/Old Carols   *Buñuelos*/Mexican Desse
Presepio/Large *Nacimiento*   Mexico & Central America's Christmas Pageant/*Las Posadas*   Christmas Eve/*Noche Buena*
Pastores/Choir Boy Procession   Pig/South American Dinner Favorite   *Dulce De Lechoze*/Dessert of Papayas

---
— 86

Have A Merry Christmas
1. Spanish   2. Danish   3. Italian   4. Norwegian   5. Dutch   6. Hungarian   7. French   8. German   9. Irish   10. Chinese   11. Finnish
12. Polish   13. Portuguese   14. Turkish   15. Afrikaans

— 88

Roots of New Year's Celebrations
ACROSS: 3. prayed   5. springtime   6. wassail   8. oldest   11. Denmark   13. calendar   14. Scotland
DOWN: 1. *strenae*   2. fourth   4. resolutions   7. Janus   9. darkness   10. faces   12. party

---
— 91

American New Year's Celebrations
1. Dutch (+t)   2. kid (+o) power   3. good (+u) luck   4. carriages (+r)   5. midnight church (+n)   6. Philadelphia (+a)   7. Mumming (+m)
8. theme (+e)   9. Indians (+n)   10. traditional (+t)   11. doo (+o) dah   12. five - half (+f)   13. Charles (+r) Holder   14. open houses (+o)
15. plays (+s)   16. flowers (+e)   17. midnight (+s)
Another name for the Rose Parade is the
tournament of roses

— 94

New Year's Celebrations Around The World
1. *Shoogatsu*   2. parties   3. testament   4. *boonenkai*   5. pig   6. *Hogmanay*   7. brooms   8. strawman   9. tree branch   10. *shimenawa*
11. footer   12. fortune   13. family   14. Temple   15. Grandpa Frost
Special New Year's Message:
i wish you and everybody in the world a happy new year

98

Epiphany

Number of Gifts: 78

```
              S w e d e n
              I t a l y
              S y r i a
      E u r o p e
  B e l g i u m
              M e x i c o
      S p a i n
```

Letters in Stars: Wisemen

— **101** —

Martin Luther King Day

ACROSS: 1. memorial 7. religious 9. equality 11. protest 12. rights 15. civil rights 16. Johnson 17. president 18. Scott
DOWN: 1. Martin Luther King 2. marches 3. life 4. boycott 5. pastor 6. college 8. brothers 10. Atlanta 13. nonviolent 14. Washington

— **106** —

Tu B'shvat

1. agricultural 2. Hebrew 3. trees 4. ancient 5. springtime 6. Jewish/symbol 7. good, strong, noble 8. cedar/cypress 9. flowers/leaves 10. fields/schools 11. fruit 12. custom/fifteenth 13. Israel 14. recreation 15. wood/conserve/shade/animals 16. U.S.

Another name for *Tu B'shvat* is:
the new year of
the trees

— **109** —

Chinese New Year

ACROSS: 1. parades 4. Dragon 5. *li* 8. Eve 10. bamboo 11. fruit 12. new 15. very 16. rice 18. *popo* 19. Only 20. *Kowtow*
DOWN: 1. part 2. dance 3. seal 6. Red 7. February 9. coins 11. Fireworks 13. *Bai* 14. money 17. crowd 20. low

— **112** —

Groundhog Day

ACROSS: 1. woodchuck 4. predictor 5. six 8. *Candlemas* 9. February 10. seven
DOWN: 2. disagree 3. Middle Ages 4. Punxsatawney 5. shadow 6. Germany 7. badger

— **114** —

Lincoln's Birthday

Abraham Lincoln was born in Kentucky on February 12, 1809.
When he was seven, Lincoln and his family moved to Indiana.
Young Abe had little chance to go to school, but he read every book he could find.
After moving to Illinois, Abe Lincoln set out on his own.
Lincoln studied law and became interested in politics.
In 1860, Abraham Lincoln was elected President of the United States.
Lincoln's Emancipation Proclamation freed the slaves in states at war with the Union.
Before he could enjoy the peace he had helped to win, President Lincoln was shot by an assassin.

— **117** —

Valentine's Day History

1. T 2. F 3. T 4. T 5. T 6. T 7. F 8. T 9. F 10. T 11. F 12. T 13. F 14. T 15. F 16. T 17. F 18. T 19. T 20. T 21. T 22. F 23. F 24. T 25. T 26. F

— **120** —

Valentine Cards And Symbols

1. symbol 2. Doves 3. purity 4. Aphrodite 5. hearts 6. Eros 7. mirror 8. beauty 9. love 10. mail 11. playful 12. intelligence 13. Pink 14. emotions 15. invisible 16. wings 17. Red 18. fifteenth 19. second 20. commercial 21. ten 22. valentines 23. writers 24. cards

Secret Valentine Message:
You are my
valentine
forever

123

Washington's Birthday
ACROSS: 1. farmhouse 4. commander 6. respect 7. colonial 10. smart 12. tutors 15. leadership 16. Virginia 17. Fox hunts
DOWN: 2. holiday 3. Federal 4. Constitution 5. tobacco 8. Custis 9. two 11. Mt. Vernon 13. surveyor 14. king

---

127

Mardi Gras
1. A 2. M 3. R 4. T 5. G 6. I 7. S 8. E 9. O 10. H 11. K 12. D 13. U 14. F 15. N 16. Y
Secret Holiday Message:
**MARDI GRAS IS HERE
TONIGHT. GET YOUR
MASK — YOU'RE OUT
OF SIGHT!**

130

Japanese Girls' Day
ACROSS: 2. gentleness 3. pride 5. March 8. *Hina Matsuri* 10. afford 11. charms 13. straw
DOWN: 1. *hishi mochi* 4. emperor 6. heirlooms 7. tea 8. human beings 9. *sokutai* 12. *amazake*

133

Saint Patrick's Day
True Statements: 1, 4, 7, 8, 9, 12, 15

136

Holi
1. U 2. R 3. P 4. A 5. L 6. Y 7. N 8. O 9. W 10. T 11. E 12. B 13. H 14. I 15. D
What would be a good business to open after *Holi*?
OPEN A LAUNDRY AND YOU WOULD NOT BE IN THE RED!

140

April Fool's Day
True Statements: 4, 5, 7, 8, 9, 10, 12, 13, 16, 17, 18, 19

143

Passover
1. Pesach (+f) 2. eight (+e) 3. April (+s) 4. herbs (+t) 5. slavery (+i) 6. Egypt (+v) 7. synagogue (+a) 8. Seder (+l) 9. matzoh (+o)
10. freedom (+f) 11. tears (+f) 12. unleavened (+r) 13. *Haggadah* (+e) 14. *afikomen* (+e) 15. questions (+d) 16. togetherness (+o)
17. Moses (+m)
**Passover is also called the
festival of freedom**

146

Easter Celebrations
England/Pace-Eggers Pretzels/Germany Russia/"XB" Cake Easter Parade/Romans Mexico/Judas *Piñata*
Bread Decorated With Eggs/Spain Eastre Festival/Teutonic Peoples *Khristukas*/Lithuania Bread Decorated With Eggs/Greece
Kulich/Alaska German Tyrol/Eggs For Carolers Eostre Festival/Anglo-Saxons Bethlehem, PA/First U.S. Sunrise Service
Hungary/Water Shower Lily/Bermuda Germany/Egg Trees Switzerland/Egg Trees

---

150

The Easter Rabbit And Easter Eggs

The first Christians to
use eggs at Easter
were the Macedonians.

Eastern Europeans
use wax to create
designs on eggs.

An old European belief
holds that the Easter rabbit
can speak on Easter day.

The rabbit
was an ancient
symbol of the moon.

German children were
told that the Easter
rabbit made his dyes
by burning wild flowers.

Eggs are not an
important part of Easter
in Spanish-speaking countries.

All over the world,
people have made dyes
with vegetables and herbs.

Swiss, German and Belgian
children hoped the Easter rabbit
would fill their nests with eggs.

152

Easter Games And Contests
True Statements:
Egg gathering in Germany is usually done with a partner.
Each year, there is an egg-rolling contest on the White House lawn.
Egyptian children roll eggs in a bowling game.

Sometimes, eggs are rolled on tracks of sticks.
In Belgium, egg gatherers are sometimes blindfolded.
English children enjoy egg hopping.
In Holland, children perform an egg dance in a large circle.
Children have enjoyed egg contests for hundreds of years.
What must you do to get a lazy Easter rabbit to run faster?
You have to egg him on!

--- 155 ---

Pan American Day
1. Brasilia 2. Chile 3. Ecuador 4. Nicaragua 5. Montevideo 6. Quito 7. Rio 8. United States

--- 158 ---

Songkran
1. A 2. D 3. T 4. H 5. O 6. E 7. N 8. W 9. P 10. S 11. I
Why did the thin man go to Thailand's Water Festival?
HE WANTED TO WHET HIS APPETITE
A. wet, spray, faucet, ice, drip
B. swim, steam, tank, leak, pour
C. wash, splash, pitcher, hose, drink

--- 162 ---

Arbor Day
1. strength 2. Nebraska 3. preservation 4. one million 5. Latin 6. states 7. J. Sterling Morton 8. bird 9. Christmas
10. important 11. England 12. forests
Nebraska's nickname is the
Tree planters

--- 165 ---

May Day
1. Roman 2. outlaw 3. Italy 4. German 5. Spain 6. morning 7. Hawaii
What did the baby maypole say to its mother when she got all wrapped up at the maypole dance?
Hi mummy!

--- 167 ---

Cinco De Mayo
1. A 2. T 3. O 4. K 5. E 6. U 7. S 8. I 9. B 10. Q 11. D 12. C
What Is The Best Shape For A *Piñata*?
A DUCK, BECAUSE IT IS QUICK TO QUACK

--- 170 ---

Tango-No-Seku
True Sentences: 1, 2, 6, 7, 9, 10, 12

--- 173 ---

Tarini Nal

Dances	Sports	Foods
Traditional circle dances	Wrestling (*sirem*)	Rice cake favors
Drum dance	Martial arts (*taekwondo*)	Korean barbecued meat
	Tug-of-war	Hot dogs
Contests		Popcorn
Painting	**Shows**	Pickled cabbage
Creative writing	Plays	**Free Entertainment**
Swings (kick the bell)	Puppet shows	Children's Park
		Movies

--- 175 ---

Pista Ng Anihan
1. Philippines...l 2. Isidro...y 3. Spanish...f 4. harvest...r 5. homes...d 6. *anoks*...h 7. bamboo...o 8. church...m
9. parade...b 10. softball...n 11. Queen...c 12. Tinikling...e 13. dancers...p 14. capture...s 15. morning...a 16. carabao...u
17. greased...g 18. *lechon*...i 19. *Bibingka*...t 20. goodies...v

215

pista ng anihan,
a time to feast
and play.
because the
harvest's
    bountiful,
they also stop
to pray.

── 178 ────────────────

Mother's Day History
1. second 2. Phrygia/Cybel 3. Romans 4. *Mater* 5. flowers 6. Mothering 7. Jarvis 8. Wilson 9. West Virginia 10. red/carnation
11. stamp
A Secret Holiday Poem
a happy
mother's day
to mothers
everywhere

sit back,
have fun,
no work,
no care.

── 181 ────────────────

Mother's Day Celebrations
ACROSS: 2. Australia 3. *Durga Puja* 4. meal 5. Christmas 9. family 10. two 11. Red Cross
DOWN: 1. happiness 2. Anna Jarvis 3. different 5. Church 6. *Materice* 7. day 8. flowers

---

── 184 ────────────────

Memorial Day
True Statements: 1, 4, 5, 7, 9, 11, 12, 13, 16
On Memorial Day, many Boy Scouts and Girl Scouts visit veterans' cemeteries and on each grave place a tiny
FLAG

── 187 ────────────────

Flag Day
1777: Bennington flag carried into battle
1814: Francis Scott Key wrote "Star Spangled Banner"
1818: Congress passed Flag Act
1824: American flag first called "Old Glory"
1870: Betsy Ross' grandson claims she made first American flag
1877: First celebration of Flag Day
1892: Pledge of Allegiance written
1949: Flag Day made official U.S. holiday
1954: Words added to Pledge of Allegiance recited

── 190 ────────────────

Father's Day
True Statements: 2, 4, 5, 6, 7, 9, 10, 11, 14, 16
DAD

── 193 ────────────────

Midsummer And St. John's Day
1. fern (+g) 2. June (+o) 3. St. John's fires (+o) 4. light (+d) 5. leaves (+l) 6. midnight sun (+u) 7. St. (+c) John's Day 8. magical (+k
9. luck (+t) 10. green (+o) 11. fjords (+y) 12. John (+o) 13. *San Juan* (+u) 14. wade (+a) 15. Flag Day (+l) 16. marry (+w)
17. costumes (+a) 18. torches (+y) 19. maypole (+s)
The Fortune-Telling Egg's Secret Holiday Message:
good luck to you always

── 197 ────────────────

Dragon Boat Festival
1. China (+f) 2. *Dyun* (+e) *Ngn Jit* 3. Ch'u Yuan (+s) 4. Mi-Lo (+t) 5. poet (+i) 6. unjust (+v) 7. prince (+a) 8. dishonorable (+l)
9. unhappy (+o) 10. moon (+f) 11. Hunan (+t) 12. boats (+h) 13. gongs (+e) 14. honor (+h) 15. rice (+i) 16. sea monster (+g) 17. silk (+h
18. dragons (+n) 19. save (+o) 20. fisherman (+o) 21. twenty fourth (+n)
Another name for the Dragon Boat Festival is
festival of the high noon

200

Dominion Day

  Green: Quebec, Ontario, Nova Scotia, New Brunswick
  Orange: Manitoba, Prince Edward Island, British Columbia
  Yellow: Alberta and Saskatchewan
  Red: Newfoundland (including Labrador)
  Brown: Northwest and Yukon territories
  Star: Detroit, Michigan / Windsor, Ontario

— 202

July 4, 1776

The first permanent English colony in America was established in 1607.
The British forced the colonists to pay taxes.
To protest the taxes, some Bostonians held a special "tea party."
The British passed laws to punish the Bostonians.
The First Continental Congress drew up a Declaration of Rights.
Battles at Lexington and Concord began America's War for Independence.
Thomas Jefferson wrote most of the Declaration of Independence.
Delegates from all the colonies signed the Declaration of Independence.
The United States won its independence.

— 204

Fourth of July Celebrations

Philadelphia, PA, July 4, 1777: Philadelphians today celebrated the first anniversary of the signing of the Declaration of Independence with bonfires, fireworks, and thirteen-gun salutes.

Philadelphia, PA, July 4, 1876: The people of Philadelphia marked America's one-hundredth birthday by hosting a world's fair filled with exhibits from around the world.

New York City, July 4, 1976: New Yorkers today watched a procession of tall-masted ships and other vessels sail up and down the Hudson River in "Operation Sail" — a Bicentennial salute to two hundred years of American independence.

Bristol, Rhode Island, July 4, 198___: Fire engine companies from all over New England today competed in Bristol's annual Independence Day water-squirting contest.

Hannibal, Missouri, July 4, 198___: Young people from all over Missouri came to Hannibal today to participate in the National Fence Painting Contest, a yearly event that highlights the town's July 4 celebrations.

Lititz, PA, July 4, 198___: The people of Lititz today celebrated July 4 by holding their annual Festival of Candles, floating thousands of lighted candles on a lake near the town.

Ontario, CA, July 4, 198___: The people of Ontario hosted the nation's biggest July 4 picnic today, with tables stretching down one of the city's major streets for a distance of two miles.

— 207

Bastille Day

  1. fourteenth   2. Bastille   3. fourth   4. Independence   5. king   6. England   7. Rights/Man   8. Declaration/Bill   9. six   10. hundred
11. *Liberté, Egalité, Fraternité*

Mystery Questions:

What was the famous cry before the American War for Independence?

Give me liberty or give me death!

Who said it?

Patrick henry of virginia